Expedition to Mystery Mountain

EXPEDITION TO MYSTERY MOUNTAIN

Adventures of a Bushwhacking, Knickerbocker-wearing Woman

SUSANNA ORESKOVIC

Walnut Tree Press
www.walnuttreepress.ca
For more information, to obtain media excerpts or to invite the author to speak at an event, please contact: info@walnuttreepress.ca

This work depicts actual events in the life of the author as truthfully as recollection permits, and as references to historical events can be verified by research. All persons within are actual individuals. Occasionally, dialogue consistent with the character of the person speaking has been supplemented.

Cover design and map illustration by Sarah Beaudin
All images by Susanna Oreskovic except where otherwise stated

ISBN 978-0-993918711 (paperback)
ISBN 978-0-993918728 (electronic)

For my dad, explorer of life.

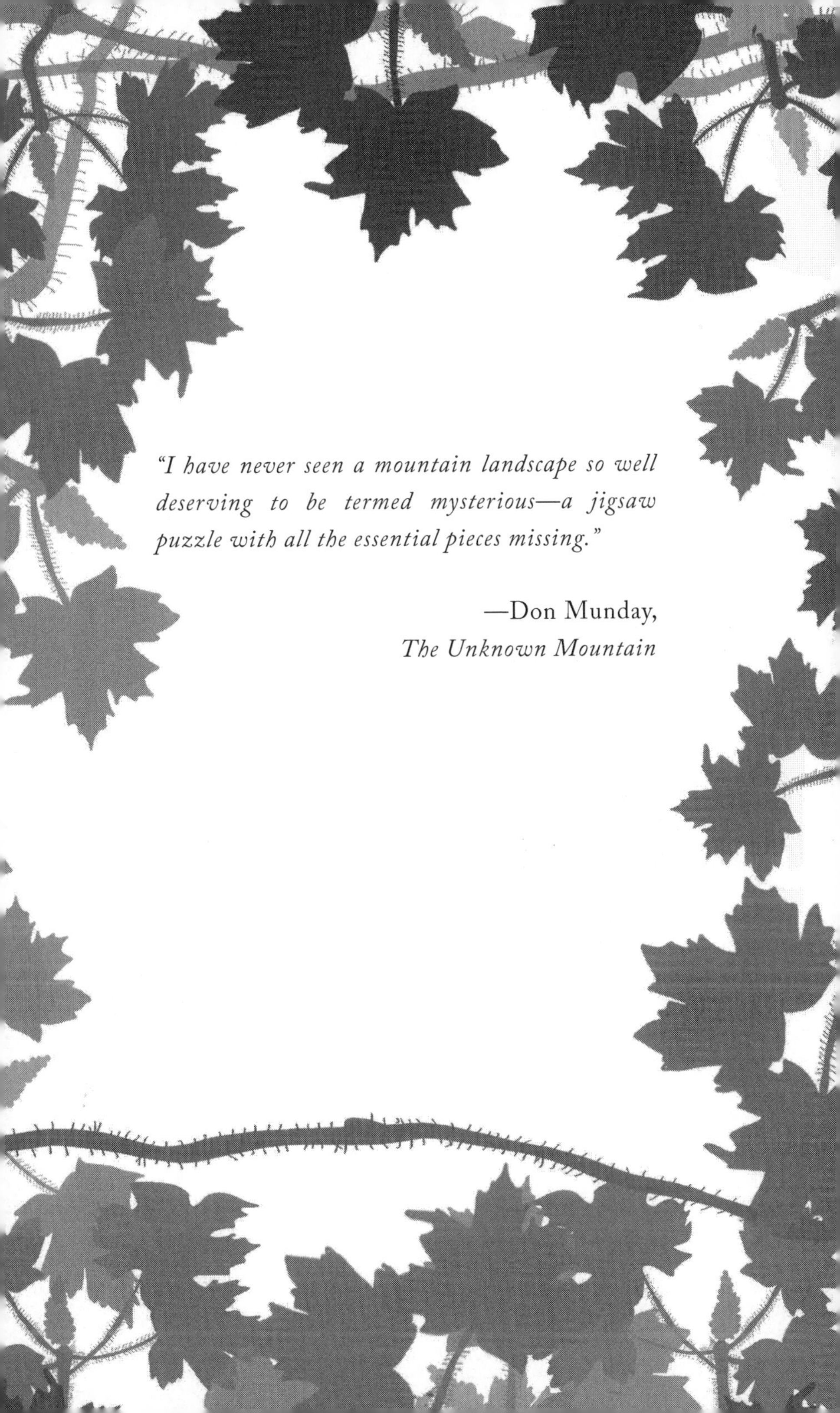

"I have never seen a mountain landscape so well deserving to be termed mysterious—a jigsaw puzzle with all the essential pieces missing."

—Don Munday,
The Unknown Mountain

Contents

Introduction

EVER SINCE I CAN REMEMBER, adventure stories of Jules Verne and Indiana Jones filled my imagination. As a girl, watching old movies of explorers going into the heart of Africa, I delighted in vicariously experiencing exotic locales and discovering how the hero overcame unexpected predicaments.

My imagination knew no bounds. I re-enacted scenes from movies with my sisters in our living room, propping up cushions for sets and using wooden spoons and bowls as props. I was constantly drawing film characters and imaginary heroines I wanted to see, like a medieval knight with long, flowing hair on a quest. I spent hours daydreaming and playing in our yard, imagining blades of grass as forests and stones as mountains.

Curiosity about what lay around the corner and the desire to see for myself was, to a degree, fostered by my mother's account of my first adventure story when I was a toddler. My family was emigrating from Croatia, where I was born, to

Australia by ocean liner. One day, as my mother was hanging laundry to dry, the ocean liner rocked unexpectedly and my dad slipped and managed to grab a post before falling overboard. Finding myself alone in the cabin, roused from my nap, I took it upon myself to drag the suitcases to the door to try to reach the handle and leave the cabin.

Eight years later we were once again on the move, bound for "Amerrrica," as my father put it to my nine-year-old self. I vividly recall studying the world map as the plane made progress toward our new home in Canada, all the while marvelling at the names of places like Fiji, Los Angeles, and Vancouver. My world was expanding.

Growing up as the daughter of immigrants, I witnessed a subtle dichotomy between my parents' traditional Croatian views of male authority and my adoptive culture's emphasis on equality between the sexes. Embracing Canadian values, I was every bit as stubborn as my father in our verbal sparring, exasperating my mother. Though I respected his judgment, I did question why his word was the final say and why my mother always took the quiet supporting role. I couldn't understand why she seemed to have less agency or wouldn't use her voice.

I was coming of age in the late 1980s, a time when young women like me were expecting to have a career in addition to taking on traditional wife and mother roles. The promise was, we could have it all if we wanted. I felt strongly that even though I was a girl I had every right to any career I wanted, even if it was unconventional. My father worked in construction, and to argue my point I declared, "You know, if I want to swing a hammer and carry two-by-fours like you, I can!"

I was audacious enough to state my desire to be unconventional but too naive to actually do it. A bright future surely lay ahead of me if I did what was expected. I sought to be a good daughter following my parents' definition of success, which meant going to university and becoming a professional. And for the next two decades, that's exactly what I did, working my way up the career ladder in top public accounting firms. But after years of committing myself to the job, working to get promoted, and adding professional titles to my name, I came to a point where more of the same held less significance. Life was more than work and I was more than my career. Defining myself solely by my profession, and later by my marital and family status, did not fulfill me as conventional ideals would have led me to believe. I recalled the joy I'd experienced when I tried rock climbing and darkroom photography in university. I longed for the freedom to explore, to travel to remote places and to be creative again. On a physical and spiritual level, I needed to nurture my inner artist and adventurer.

By the early 2000s I'd adopted the moniker *mountain woman*, mainly for myself and to myself. It personified an alter ego very different from the workaholic professional I had been living as up to that point. I returned to darkroom photography, where my subjects of choice were landscapes and the natural world. To take my projects further afield, I honed my mountaineering skills with week-long courses in the Rockies and Coast Mountains of British Columbia. Closer to home, I learned technical rope skills while rock climbing on the Laurentian cliffs north of Montreal. I was searching for people who, like me, were passionate, nature-loving, and adventurous, and I finally found them at the Alpine Club of

Canada, our national mountaineering association. Almost immediately upon joining my local branch of the Alpine Club, I was organizing its first photography contest. By the following year I was leading the Montreal chapter.

Without meaning to, I happened to become the first elected female president of the Montreal section's forty-year history. Women and men had been fairly equally represented across national membership ranks of the club since 1906, so I wondered why this kind of milestone was still happening in the twenty-first century.

At weekly club socials, members presented slide shows of their mountain adventures. Sure enough, if there were any women in the team, there was only one. I couldn't explain why there were fewer women leading trips and hardly any women-only climbs. When I read a book about the first all-women expedition to the Himalayas in 1955, I was amazed at their temerity. The three women had spent nine months planning their trip, and I sympathized when they revealed that the preparations often conflicted with their professional and domestic duties.[1] They were keenly aware of the scrutiny they would endure simply for being female should any mishap occur during their trip. Women like these were curious and bold enough to explore the farthest reaches of the earth even though by convention their place was at home with family. I began collecting stories of adventurous women throughout history for my bookshelf. These accounts were deep wells of inspiration connecting me to women who'd come before.

Women explorers being altogether less well known than their male counterparts, my attention perked up whenever I came across a historical account of a female mountaineer.

One weekend at the Alpine Club refuge for rock climbers in Ontario's Bon Echo Provincial Park, I became entranced upon speaking with a fellow climber and history aficionado named Bryan Thompson, whose twinkling eyes and jovial disposition brought to life the story of Phyllis Munday. Phyllis was as accomplished as a man in mountain climbing and has often been described to be as strong as one too. She spent her youth learning camping skills with her Girl Guide troop and developed climbing expertise when she joined the British Columbia Mountaineering Club in 1915, and later, the Alpine Club of Canada.[2] She and her husband Don formed an inseparable couple who, in the decade from 1926 to 1936, explored much of the unmapped Waddington Range in the Coast Mountains of BC. They lived in a log cabin north of Vancouver and earned their living from Don's writing about their mountaineering discoveries, to which Phyllis supplied photographs taken with her Kodak camera.[3] The articles were published in newspapers and journals in Canada, the US, and Britain.

It was on a hike on Vancouver Island that the Mundays first spotted what they believed was a peak taller than Mount Robson, the then-accepted highest peak in BC at 12 972 feet (3954 metres). In the words of Don Munday: "The compass showed [that] the alluring peak stood along a line passing a little east of Bute Inlet . . . where blank spaces on the map left ample room for many nameless mountains. It was . . . destiny beckoning . . . a torch to set the imagination on fire."[4] They named this alluring peak Mystery Mountain, Don estimating its elevation at 13 000 feet. Geographical surveys later confirmed that Mystery Mountain, now officially named

Mount Waddington, does in fact measure 13 186 feet (4019 metres). Similar in relief to the Himalayas, Mount Waddington continues to be notoriously remote and difficult to access.

Bryan explained his big plans to me. "I'm putting a team together for a five-week expedition to recreate the Mundays' initial route to Mount Waddington. We'll do it the same way they did, you know, hobnail boots, wooden pack frames, wool sleeping bags, hemp climbing rope. I'm looking for a woman to take on the role of Phyllis Munday. You'd be perfect."

Intrigued and flattered, I responded, "Sounds great, but why use period-style gear?"

"We've lost something that people had a hundred years ago," Bryan said, a dreamy look beginning to glaze his eyes. "They went out there in uncharted territory without the conveniences we rely on today. No lightweight packs, no waterproof clothing, no GPS." His hands grasping something ethereal, he went on, "They had resilience, self-sufficiency, strength of character. The spirit of adventure. I want to experience what it must have been like for these early explorers."

The way to Mystery Mountain has become legendary among climbers, not only for the challenge of scaling the highest mountain that stands entirely within BC, but for the particularly difficult route to its base through the Homathko River Valley. In this temperate coniferous rainforest, massive hemlocks and Douglas firs tower above while the understorey is thick with shrubs, including the prehistoric-looking devil's club. Some opt to bypass the valley and be flown by helicopter to the mountain, or else access the peak by way of the Franklin Glacier, which the Mundays did in 1928. An enterprising crew of professional athletes from the outdoor clothing and adventure company Arc'teryx attempted in 2016 to recreate the Mundays' 1926 route through the Homathko River Valley.

"It would be something if we could nail this route where the Arc'teryx team couldn't," Bryan mused.

Outfitted with light, modern gear, maps, and GPS devices, the Arc'teryx team lasted only three weeks before internal dissent overtook them and they called in a helicopter to pluck them out of the bush and carry them to the mountain.

Bryan purposefully did not present the trip as all sunshine and rainbows. "It's going to be a tough slog with plenty of misery," he warned me. "You'll have to carry a heavy load. We're likely to encounter bears and quicksand, get rained on, and battle with the thorny devil's club bush." My pulse quickened and I signed up. So did Stuart Rickard and Joe Vanasco, who were at the climbers' refuge at Bon Echo that weekend.

A few weeks later, I called Bryan to say, "You won't believe this, but I found an authentic 1921 Kodak camera. I'm going to use it to take photos like Phyllis did." He reacted with such excitement, I could practically see him grinning ear to ear through the phone.

Finding a vintage camera hadn't been as difficult as I'd thought because the early 1900s had given rise to an explosion of portable consumer cameras manufactured by the Eastman Kodak Company. The challenge was to find a working camera that used a film format that was still being produced. Taking a chance on the choices online, I purchased a 1921 Kodak No. 2 Autographic that seemed to be in good condition. It was similar to the camera Phyllis Munday had used, although about half the size. At a local photo store I bought a box of 120 mm film, a format over three times bigger than today's typical 35 mm. After cleaning the mould off the lens and patching up the holes in the accordion-shaped bellows, my Kodak functioned beautifully. It would serve on the expedition as a supplement to my digital camera—I was willing to sacrifice some authenticity to guarantee decent photographs.

The nine months that followed were a blur of intense preparations, phone calls, and vintage store finds. We procured grants and sponsors and held fundraising events to help finance the expedition. Bryan researched the route, speaking with mountaineers who had knowledge of the area, and chartered a vintage-style boat to set us off on the journey like the Mundays, who travelled by steamship to the mouth of the Homathko River before starting on foot toward the mountain. Bryan also visited library archives to find the Mundays' packing lists as well as their photographs and film reels, from which we could get a visual on how to construct our gear. In the 1920s, camping equipment was expensive or non-existent. Don designed the tents and sleeping bags himself and constructed wood-frame packs from alder and canvas while Phyllis did the sewing and food preparation.[5] Our team was going to do the same.

Working solely from the photographs Bryan had unearthed, Joe designed and sewed two A-frame tents. Though tent manufacturers of the 1920s typically used heavy cotton canvas, the Mundays had chosen cotton sailcloth for its light weight and water resistance. The fabric was extremely difficult to find because boating suppliers stopped selling it in the 1950s, switching to Dacron (a type of polyester) instead. We finally managed to secure just enough sailcloth from a local historian who was an expert in traditional materials.

While Joe was taking care of tents, Stuart was in charge of sleeping bags. Scouring vintage shops, he found one Woods Arctic Eiderdown sleeping bag, first invented in 1898—and we needed six. Using it as a model, he constructed the rest from down duvets lined with wool army blankets. He sewed on snaps around the edges because zippers were not yet widely in use in the 1920s except on rubber galoshes.[6] Our reconstructed Eiderdowns were just as warm as modern sleeping bags but three times heavier at ten pounds each.

To prepare my body for the extra weight of the vintage gear and the challenging terrain, I committed to six months of strength training with a Polish coach nicknamed the Beast from the East. I figured if I was going to haul antique camping gear down the trail every day, I had better train just as often.

A number of times before the trip, I was asked what my family and kids would do without me for a month, or what could possibly motivate me to give up the comforts of home to risk my life in a bear-infested forest with a bunch of sweaty men. Beneath these concerns lay an implicit bias about what constitutes an acceptable risk for women. I can't imagine that many male mountaineers are questioned about their children or admonished for taking on a project that involves a degree of danger. Theirs would be for the glory of the endeavour. I had no wish to put my life in peril. But I did want to try something new, witness landscapes that few people had ever seen, and take photographs of those vistas. This was an adventure. Why would anyone pass that up?

Traditionally, mountaineering culture has scrutinized women who pushed beyond their expected roles and took on risks. Phyllis Munday avoided some scrutiny by climbing with her husband Don, who treated her as an equal, but the same could not be said of the other members of their expedition parties. "For many men," Phyllis's biographer Kathryn Bridge wrote, "the mention of a woman climbing with them would be met with grumbling and resentment."[7] Decades later, women climbers are commonplace, yet many elite female mountaineers are still beset by criticism and held to higher standards than men. For instance, the summit accomplishments of a team of women climbers in the Himalayas were questioned as qualifying as all-female because they included the support of male Sherpas.[8] Would an American mountaineering feat be considered any less for including Nepalese guides?

Less than 10 per cent of those who have summited the world's highest mountains, such as Everest and K2, are women. It's a familiar story, whether on the tallest mountain peaks or in senior executive boardrooms: women hold a fraction of the top positions. I can't help thinking that the competitive and individualist values by which we measure success may be part of the issue.

Women have been adventuring long before society deemed it acceptable, and their stories are out there if you look for them. In writing the book *Savage Summit*, about the first five female mountaineers to climb K2 (between 1986 and 1995), author Jennifer Jordan's motivation was to give women their due credit: "Books and memoirs were mostly about men, and women mountaineers seemed to be a footnote in climbing history."[9] Jordan remarks that it was challenging to research these women, who despite their achievements had such poorly recorded histories that not one summit photo could be found.

Mountaineering literature has long favoured the male point of view. A recent study surveying climbers' autobiographies written since the early nineteenth century found that women's perspectives account for 6 per cent of all stories compared to 94 per cent authored by men, *despite almost equal numbers in alpine club membership ranks.*[10] Women's stories deserve to be told, not kept locked away in personal journals. We as women need to use our voices and show that our experiences are as worthy, as exciting, as meaningful as men's.

My aim in writing *Expedition to Mystery Mountain* is to honour the women who have come before me and inspire those who will come after. My hope is that you'll give yourself permission to try something new, celebrate the attempt, learn from failure, and by all means, share your own story.

—Susanna

Chapter One

The First Glitch

THE BUBBLE-GUM PINK princess lunch box dangling from Stuart's hand seemed curiously out of place against his brown wool knickerbockers. Not quite standard issue in 1926, I thought, watching from my perch on the rear bulkhead of the *Misty Isles*. Borrowed from his six-year-old daughter, the compact box housed Stuart's new aerial drone. He took a wide step off the deck of the schooner into an inflatable Zodiac raft, followed by Greg with his video camera. The drone was going to fly overhead to capture a bird's-eye view of the *Misty Isles* on the majestic fjord while Greg filmed wide-angle shots of the boat. The footage was sure to be striking, the 43-foot schooner's distinctive red sails unfurled against the backdrop of the towering mountains.

The 2018 expedition team sails on the Misty Isles *schooner along the majestic Bute Inlet, which carves its way inland from the west coast of British Columbia. The eighty-kilometre journey would take nine hours to reach Homathko Camp, deep in the interior.*

Our expedition to Mystery Mountain had begun early that morning, July 5, 2018. We'd embarked from Quadra Island, one of the pockets of land that dot the inside passage between Vancouver Island and mainland British Columbia. Excitement and expectation had hung in the air as we prepared to leave the lodge we'd slept at. Guests gathered along the dock, some still in their pyjamas, others with coffee cup in hand, to watch the spectacle of six climbers dressed in 1926-style woollen clothes and felt hats emerge from the lodge and walk up the gangway to the old schooner. Even though the faces of the well-wishers were unfamiliar, they reminded me of the family and friends we were leaving behind. We waved goodbye as our skipper, Captain Mike, steered us away from the dock.

On the surrounding islands, rooflines peeking through the trees and floating docks jutting out from the shoreline were the only giveaways of the clusters of chalets and luxury homes hidden within. Buoys kept watch, guiding boats through the channels. We headed northeast through the passage between Maurelle and Read Islands. The channel narrowed to a scant hundred metres wide, allowing us to glimpse pictographs of faces etched in red ochre on a granite rock face. A message left over a century ago, reverberating through time to remind us that First Nations peoples had lived here long before us and the Western explorers we were emulating.

Ahead of us, snow-capped mountains floated in the distance above green forested mounds rising out of the glassy water. Almost an hour into our voyage, one of the last sign-posts of civilization we saw unassumingly identified *Stuart Island.*

"Hey, Stuart's got an island," I heard a voice behind me say, and we chuckled.

Rounding past Stuart's small mass of land, the width of the channel expanded to four kilometres and we entered the scenic fjord of Bute Inlet. The mountains enveloped us, the frosty peaks disappearing into the sky at 9000 feet (2700 metres), their forested toes dipping into the frigid waters.

It was hard to believe we were surrounded by the same rugged mountains, breathing in the same glacier-cooled air as the young couple of Don and Phyllis Munday when their expedition party set sail by steamship in 1926. It would be the first of their many forays into the unmapped Coast Mountain ranges that lay approximately three hundred kilometres northwest of Vancouver. The Mundays' legacy would be to lift the shroud of mystery that lay over the Coast Mountains to reveal towering rock summits and vast valleys of ice that were not believed to exist at the time.[1]

The Munday party aboard the steamship Venture *on Bute Inlet, 1926.* Left to Right: *R. C. (Johnnie) Johnson, Athol Agur, Thomas Ingram, Albert (Bert) Munday, Phyllis Munday, and Don Munday. Image I-51589 courtesy of the Royal BC Museum.*

Our expedition team mirrored the Mundays' original party of six in their first exploration of Mystery Mountain. Bryan Thompson, Stuart Rickard, Joe Vanasco, Ron Ireland, Patrick McGuire, and I were on a mission to recreate the 1926 expedition using entirely vintage-style gear. Greg Gransden was following along to document our five-week adventure.

The 2018 expedition party ready to set sail on the Misty Isles *schooner.* Left to Right: *Joe Vanasco, Patrick (Paddy) McGuire, Bryan Thompson, Susanna Oreskovic, Ron Ireland, and Stuart Rickard. Photo by Greg Gransden.*

Two additional climbers, Mark Hurst and Ron Rusk, would be taking a helicopter directly to the mountain and meeting us on the glacier to act as our safety support team. Except for Bryan and Ron I., who'd known each other for ages, we had all only recently met through the Alpine Club of Canada.

The day was bright but remained cloudy, the sun unable to break through, and I could feel the dampness in the air. I looked up at the sky to assess how long the rain would hold off, hoping Stuart would have enough time to fly the drone. His tall, lanky frame was folded in the rear of the raft as he unzipped the lunch box. The drone had been a lavish spend, but he'd figured if he was ever going to splurge for one, this adventure would make it worthwhile. Stuart represented Don Munday in the re-enactment, a logical choice considering their similarity in build and temperament. In his late thirties, Stuart had been raised on a farm, where he'd learned bushcraft and wilderness survival skills. His youthful looks, golden-blond hair, and clear blue eyes did not immediately reveal his resourcefulness and quiet leadership.

Expedition leader Bryan Thompson, typically seen with his pipe, surveys the landscape from the Misty Isles.

Bryan, wearing a newsboy cap and cradling a pipe, was standing by the deck railing as puffs of smoke wafted away in the breeze. As expedition leader, he had enticed each of us to join up with animated stories of the Mundays' exploits. "The Mundays were looking for a way to Mystery Mountain, the tallest peak," he'd told us the year before at the Bon Echo climbing refuge. "Some people don't realize the Waddington Range is made up of about twenty peaks over ten thousand feet high. It's a massive area," he said, swinging his arms in a wide circle for emphasis. "At one point, right when they were getting close, they realized they had only four days' worth of food left. They didn't turn around but stuck it out in a *thirty-one hour climb* to the mountain." Pausing a moment, he added, "Man, they were really tough."

A relaxed smile crossed Bryan's face as he puffed, his gaze directed at the distant mountains. He seemed content, as if absorbing every minute of being a 1920s explorer. Recently fifty, he was passionate about history and often said he'd been born in the wrong century. Representing Bert Munday, brother to Don, he was dressed in grey woollen pants, a cream collarless grandfather shirt, and an oatmeal-coloured vest. Seeing the confident way he carried himself in his outfit, I thought he was a perfect fit for the part. I quickly pulled out my digital camera from its bag and snapped a few shots.

One important task I had on this expedition was to take photographs as Phyllis Munday had done, to document the mountain landscapes and offer proof of what we'd found. I was looking forward to capturing sweeping vistas of icefields and the graceful forms of glaciers. For my 1921 Kodak camera, I had ten rolls of film that held just eight frames each—and only if I managed not to waste a frame by overwinding the manual knob. Shooting with film was a slow, methodical process, so the antique Kodak would not be the first camera I'd reach for. Its modern cousin would ensure that I'd come away with a good number of quality photographs.

Taking on Phyllis's role would require more than a vintage camera. I hoped to emulate her stoicism and courageousness, but I felt that I was nothing like her. She was as tall as most men, and I was the smallest member of the team. She was outgoing and sociable yet unassuming. Her love of the mountains brought her inexpressible joy, and she took difficulties in stride as being simply the way of life in the wilderness. A few years before her death, Phyllis was asked in an interview what people in the 1920s thought about women scampering up the mountainside, to which she replied: "I don't know and I don't think I particularly cared as long as I could go."[2] She did not view herself as a role model for gender equality.[3] In the mountains she was simply a climber.

My Phyllis-inspired attire included a vintage pair of olive knickerbocker pants that ended at the knees, graciously loaned to me by an Alpine Club member. In Phyllis's time, women hikers had only recently gained the freedom to trade in their long, cumbersome skirts for men's knickerbockers, or knickers, thanks to sweeping social changes after the end of World War I. This pant style had been popular among cyclists, golfers, and skiers since the late 1800s. Phyllis sewed her own knickers out of old blankets made of wool, a warm yet breathable material whose natural oils imparted water resistance.[4] Covering my lower legs were a pair of long socks, then khaki-coloured leg wrappings called *puttees*—long, narrow strips of wool used like gaiters to provide protection and support. Puttees had first been adopted by the British Army in India, who'd borrowed the practice from local tribal dress as a cheaper alternative to tall leather boots.[5] On my feet were men's leather oxfords from a thrift store. To ward off the cool breeze as we sailed, I wore a wool sweater over my grey denim shirt. A red silk scarf like Phyllis's was the finishing touch, neatly tied around my neck and dancing in the wind.

Having taken photos of Bryan, my camera was itching to see what the others were up to. I stood up from my perch to explore the ship. Stuart's drone was hovering somewhere above the fjord, tiny and imperceptible like an insignificant insect. I walked past the wheelhouse toward the bow, where the Zodiac was circling around in front of us. Jutting out over the water was the pointed bowsprit, with Patrick sprawled out in its rope netting as if he were the ship's figurehead, though he bore little resemblance to a carved wooden mermaid. I lifted my camera and took a shot.

"Hey there, Phyllis," he greeted me jovially.

"Hey, Paddy, what ya doing lollygagging up there?" I said.

Patrick finds an ideal spot to lounge on the bowsprit of the Misty Isles.

"Catching some Z's if you please," he replied, cocking his head back and placing his newsboy cap over his eyes.

At fifty-six he was the eldest of our group, yet there was a lighthearted, boyish humour about him. Stocky, with arms and legs like baseball bats, he looked as strong as a horse. Of the Munday party Patrick represented Johnnie Johnson, who, with Athol Agur, battled the almost impassable Homathko River by canoe, carrying supplies for the group.

Greg Gransden, the filmmaker following the expedition, takes a tour on the Zodiac raft to begin shooting his documentary. Photo by Stuart Rickard.

I turned to photograph the steeply rising mountains layered on top of one another, their running gullies forming unique wrinkles across each plane. Below, the Zodiac was gliding in parallel with the sailboat. Greg's face was eclipsed by his video camera directed at the snoozing figurehead and me. His wavy black hair stood out against his red Gore-Tex jacket. In his late forties, Greg was not part of the historical re-enactment team. He wasn't expected to lug a heavy wood-frame pack around, nor to cook or chop wood. His main job was to capture our progress on film for the documentary he was producing. Soft-spoken and unobtrusive, he quietly blended into the background, observing.

Joe sauntered toward Patrick and me, sandwich in hand. He plopped himself down in the sheltered space between the front of the wheelhouse and the bow.

"If you guys are hungry, there's sandwiches," he called out. "You better eat up. I, for one, am going to enjoy this little luxury."

Joe was a gregarious, extroverted guy with the gift of gab—he'd talk to himself if no one else was around. And he'd tell it like he saw it. In his early forties, he was younger than his historical counterpart, Thomas Ingram, who at fifty was about to retire from climbing when the Mundays asked him to join them. Like Thomas, Joe was not quite tall, had dark eyes, and could be forgetful. His handsome facial features and thick black hair gave away his Italian roots.

The wind at the bow was starting to feel chilly. The saturated clouds were hanging low, obscuring the distant peaks. A light drizzle began and I reached for my rain jacket, which we'd waterproofed with beeswax. The Zodiac was now out of sight as it had circled back behind the sailboat. The weather must have forced them to return, I thought. I made my way toward the stern to seek shelter in the wheelhouse. Stuart and Greg emerged on deck, looking rather solemn. Stuart locked eyes with Bryan.

"We lost the drone," he stated quietly.

"Oh Stu, I'm so sorry," Bryan sympathized. "Didn't that cost you something like nine hundred dollars?"

A knowing look was all that was exchanged. The drone was irretrievable. Once its trajectory had faltered, it had simply slipped below the dark grey water, where it was now sinking two thousand feet down to the bottom of the fjord. It was a great financial loss, but the disappearance of that spectacular footage was even more lamentable.

Looking to the rest of the team, Bryan quipped, "Well, there's our first glitch," hoping to hearten our long faces.

The deck was glistening with moisture that reflected the grey sky. I located the hatch behind the wheelhouse that led below deck into the hold, where I hoped to find a bathroom. Among the boxes and piles of gear Ron was curled up, trying to rest. I moved quietly past him. Ron, also fifty, was Bryan's long-time friend, and counterbalanced our leader's ambitious ideas with skepticism and practicality. A firefighter by trade, he was familiar with taking calculated risks and relied on careful planning. Broad-shouldered and towering tall above me, he was our strongest man. Though he represented Athol Agur of the Munday party, just now Ron looked more like a hobo who had stolen away in the boat, his shabby wool jacket and felt hat covering his face. I didn't know if it was the motion of the ship or something else that had made him find a place to lie down.

On my way back topside Ron followed me up, roused by my presence in the small hold or the noise of the latrine. Emerging from the dark hold, the sky didn't seem any brighter. Rain was still falling. We scurried through the doorway of the wheelhouse, where the others had also sought refuge, and squeezed into the L-shaped dining cubby alongside Stuart and Joe. The interior was panelled with yellow cedar, an aromatic conifer native to the Pacific Northwest coast.

Facing the postcard-sized table was the galley kitchen with an even smaller counter. Large windows offered a view of the mountains, blurred by the raindrops trickling down the panes. Patrick was sitting on the green Aztec-patterned captain's bench while Greg stood beside him with his camera at the ready.

Joe, Stuart, Susanna, and Ron listen to the safety briefing in the galley of the wheelhouse. Photo by Greg Gransden.

As the weather had us conveniently corralled together, Bryan stepped into his expedition leader role. "Hey, guys, this is a good time for the safety briefing. I want to go over the extraction plan."

I perked up my ears attentively. It irked me that we were first getting wind of this as we were already heading in. Contingency plans are usually thought out before getting a trek underway. Either Bryan had come up with them at the last minute or he felt he didn't need to involve the others in the discussion. In any case, there was nothing to do but listen.

Bryan pulled out a topographical map from his jacket pocket and laid it on the table. In our preparatory meetings we had decided that our route was not going to match the Mundays' exactly. While they had followed the western bank of the Homathko River toward Mystery Mountain, we'd be proceeding along its eastern side, where we expected old logging roads to make our hike easier. The roads connected to three key bridges over fast-running glacial rivers: the Heakamie, the Jewakwa, and the Homathko. Bryan figured we could use this infrastructure to reach the toe of the Waddington glacier in ten days—three days faster than the Mundays. Then we'd meet up with Mark and Ron R. for the climb to the summit. Our safety support team would guide Greg as he was filming and come to our rescue if needed. Overall, we had two weeks to get to the mountain, a one-week window to climb it, and two weeks to hike back out again.

The space in the wheelhouse was so tight, Bryan practically hovered over us to point to three spots on the map.

"There are three places we can get a helicopter in if anything goes sideways: Here at Homathko Camp, the start of our hike. They have a helipad and phone access. Next, there's an abandoned landing strip at the foot of Scar Mountain fifty kilometres up the valley. Then once we're over Scar Mountain, we have about twenty kilometres of glacier travel up Mount Waddington. A chopper could land almost anywhere on the glacier."

Ron's broad hands retraced the extraction route. "So if something happens, worst-case scenario, we need to be able to hike twenty-five kilometres to get to a landing site either ahead of us or behind us," he said in his smooth, velvety voice.

"Yeah, if we're in the valley," Bryan agreed.

"How are we going to call a chopper?" Joe said, even though he already knew the answer. Asking questions seemed to be his way of reviewing details for the sake of quieter members of the group, myself included.

"Since Greg isn't a re-enactor, he'll be carrying a SPOT satellite communication device," Bryan replied. "It has GPS tracking, so we'll be able to send our coordinates and text short messages to our field coordinator, Renee. She'll be our liaison to report our progress to friends and supporters, and she'll also arrange any logistics for us."

It made me feel more secure, knowing that we had this technology to connect to the outside world and call for help if needed. I wondered if I would be allowed to send a birthday message. I was going to be missing the fourteenth birthday of my eldest daughter.

Laughter around me brought my attention back to the meeting. I hadn't quite caught Joe's next question. Glancing at me out of the corner of his eye, Bryan was saying, "If the bear spray doesn't work, we've got fearless Phyl here. She'll fight off those grizzlies."

I felt my body tense up. *Oh man, eventually these guys are going to figure out I'm nothing like Phyllis.* With her ice axe, she'd once rushed to scare off a bear that was confronting Don.[6] I looked at the men around me and managed to force a smile in response to their cocky banter.

"And don't forget, we need to keep a lookout for the dangers on the List of Doom," Joe said. "Devil's club thorns, slippery moss, log crossings, quicksand. We all have to know what we're getting into."

There was levity as long as the dangers were far removed. The chatter amongst the guys went on and I opened my journal. I remembered reading the five-page List of Doom, written for us by an Alpine Club member from Vancouver. It enumerated the multitude of dangers we were likely to encounter in the Homathko River Valley and on the glaciers. Among them was getting ensnarled in tangled masses of old deadfall and dense regrowth that would require machetes to hack through. The List warned us to watch out for team members who are hungry, thirsty, or tired as these stressors can lead to poor decision-making. The Mundays themselves knew that trust in climbing partners is paramount. They had explored mountains together for a good decade before they attempted Mystery Mountain. After a particularly difficult and dangerous climb up Mount Robson, which accorded Phyllis the honour of being the first woman to reach its summit in 1924, she and Don were convinced that the mishaps caused by others in the party would not have occurred if they had been climbing together on the same rope, with hand-picked companions they could trust.[7]

I felt a familiar sensation creeping up, which in my mind looked like a blank, black void. I could not envision what we might stumble upon in the expedition, nor how our group would manage the inevitable challenges that awaited us. Could I trust in these men for my safety when danger was at hand? Would any of us succumb to fatigue and stress and put the others' lives in peril? The rain drummed on the roof of the wheelhouse. Everyone around me, the sailboat and the mountains outside—all suddenly seemed surreal, as if I were in a story. *Am I even here?* I asked myself. The pen balancing between my fingers tapped on the paper, ready to accept the words I gave it to write. But words eluded me.

Finally, in an act of relinquishing control, I scribbled: *Accept what comes.*

Chapter Two

The Edge of Civilization

I COULD SENSE TIME SLOWING DOWN and rolling back as we sailed through the day. We were time travellers, destination 1926—only instead of a time machine with knobs and blinking lights, we had a sailboat gliding gracefully on the silvery water. Forested mountains rose precipitously from the water, undulating at five thousand feet high. I could almost imagine them unfurling themselves like spring ferns into mythical protectors of this land. Surging up even taller behind them, frosted peaks blanketed by icefields looked deceptively inviting, as if topped with whipped cream.

Snow-capped mountains rise steeply on either side of Bute Inlet.

Nine hours we sailed and eighty kilometres inland to reach the head of Bute Inlet, where the Homathko River emptied. Captain Mike dropped anchor and announced, "That's as far as I can go. Homathko Camp is about four kilometres up the river. I'll take you by raft."

For their part, the Mundays had taken a small gas-powered boat up the Homathko River, no more than eleven kilometres upstream. Thereafter, the river was too treacherous to continue by boat.

From the deck of the schooner I scanned the perimeter of the shoreline, searching for a hint of civilization—a boat, a post, powerlines, anything—but found nothing. What I saw was the natural architecture of the mountains, their massive weight vaulted into the earth. I was struck with a sensation of smallness. The air that filled my lungs was sweet and fresh, carrying with it hints of hemlock and spruce. The gentle breeze whispered to me, *You are here at last.* I was about to enter the wilderness. As a city dweller I was exposed, unaccustomed to the total self-reliance that would be required of me here. Yet the trees, rocks, and rivers felt familiar from my past experiences with hiking and primitive camping.

A flurry of activity began as Joe and Patrick pulled our boxes of gear and food from the hold onto the deck. First, our wood-frame backpacks, tents, and sleeping bags. Then, bins of 1920s climbing and safety equipment. Brown leather boots, the soles reinforced with hobnails for traction. Hand-forged iron crampons with leather straps and teeth at least two inches long, looking like medieval torture devices. Vintage wooden-stemmed ice axes, longer and heavier than the modern kind, to use as anchor points on steep slopes. Hemp ropes to link us together and protect us from falls while traversing glaciers. Vintage glacier goggles. We'd use a machete, hand saw, and hatchet to chop wood. An old white tin with a red cross would serve as our first aid kit, though Greg carried a larger modern one as well.

Our cookware was heavy and bulky, unlike the compact, collapsible campware that today's backpackers use. We'd brought two large metal pots and a cast iron skillet, wooden cutting boards, enamel plates, bowls, and cups, and metal cutlery. We also had a blue enamel coffee pot, a teapot, and ten vintage military-style canteens.

Cardboard boxes and cotton sacks of gear piled into the Zodiac raft that will take the expedition members to Homathko Camp.

Most of our provisions had been purchased the day before we set sail. The types of foods we chose were the same that were available to the Mundays—no prepackaged freeze-dried meals for us. In addition to a five-week supply of tinned corned beef, baked beans, and tuna, we bought dry staples such as oatmeal, pasta, rice, lentils, and sixty pounds of flour, plus a miscellany of nuts and chocolate. Our single bag of corn flakes wouldn't survive long enough for us to eat before being reduced to crumbs. From a butcher we secured fifty pounds of cured bacon and summer sausage, chosen because it needed no refrigeration to keep. Fresh eggs, sandwich meats, and smoked ham hocks would be eaten first. We'd repackaged foods like peanut butter, lard, and butter into gallon-sized tins, and coffee and tea into smaller vintage tins. All of this was packed in large cardboard boxes we'd gotten at a supermarket. Our personal belongings, such as clothing, toiletries, and sleeping bags, were contained in cotton drawstring sacks and pillowcases.

Joe and Patrick continued to haul up boxes and bins from the hold as Stuart and Greg loaded the rafts. "Man, I don't know how we're going to pack all this food. I don't think we waterproofed enough sacks," Joe said, shaking his head.

Joe salutes Stuart as he embarks on the Zodiac. Photo by Greg Gransden.

Canned foods would keep indefinitely but were heavy; bulk staples were susceptible to spoiling from moisture. Since plastic packaging wasn't yet in use in the 1920s, Phyllis stored foods such as flour, rolled oats, rice, sugar, butter, and cheese in cotton canvas sacks that she waterproofed herself.[1] We had reproduced her system, melting beeswax and linseed oil in a pot, then rubbing the yellow liquid into the fabric. Phyllis stowed the sacks in wooden boxes to further protect them from rain and animal pilferage.[2] These boxes could easily be secured to the Mundays' pack frames. For all our preparations, the best we had was a handful of waxed cotton sacks and cardboard produce boxes that, in the rain, would soon turn to mush.

The two rafts were now laden to capacity with boxes, bins, and assorted sacks. An open box holding cooking equipment teetered on top. Stuart and Greg squeezed into one raft with the deckhand, and Ron went with Captain Mike in the other. The two rafts drifted toward the mouth of the Homathko River, looking miniscule against the theatre of the mountains before they disappeared into the bush.

Soon to be engulfed by the forest, the rafts head toward the mouth of the Homathko River.

The cloudy sky dulled the late afternoon light, dissolving any shadows. The day was getting long. Bryan, Joe, Patrick, and I remained on board the *Misty Isles*, waiting for the rafts to return for the second load. In those quiet moments, seeing the water lap against the hull of the boat, cajoling, inviting, I had the sensation of being on the edge between two realities. The moment I'd leave the boat would be my first step toward the fearless woman I'd have to become to brave the boundless wilderness. I was leaving the security of home and family. Here at what seemed like the end of the world, the intense events of the past month came rushing to the forefront of my mind. My father had recently become ill and passed away, and the tragedy had pulled my family together. I couldn't shake the feeling that I was running out on my mother, my husband, my three kids. They were supportive, but I knew they felt some degree of trepidation about my adventure. *What if something happens to me?* This was not a thought I wanted to entertain.

Soon enough, the rafts reappeared from the bush and cruised toward us, their loads lightened. Once the first raft had pulled up alongside the sailboat, Joe and Patrick replenished its stores, then jumped in. The second raft floated into position. Bryan and I packed in the remainder of our gear, and Bryan took a seat among the boxes. I gave one last glance at the deck of the schooner. It showed no trace of us, as if we hadn't been there at all. Turning back to the raft below and letting go of the handrail, I took the leap.

The reverberating hum of the motor and the swishing of the water seemed to fade before the unfolding scene. I was spellbound. Before us stood a solid wall of foliage that didn't look to hold any entryway into the river. But then a small hundred-metre opening appeared as if the forest had conceded to take us in. And there we were on the Homathko River, winding our way up an S-shaped passage. The water was milky with hints of greenish-grey rock flour made by grinding glaciers. The river would eventually stretch 144 kilometres into the interior, swelling and thinning according to the glacier melt season. Tall dark green conifers standing guard along the riverbank captured my attention as the motor droned on. I could almost picture myself as an intrepid explorer entering a hidden village, like in the many movies I had watched as a child.

The landing dock at Homathko Camp emerges from the fog drifting on the river.

As the river widened, the valley slowly revealed itself to show distant white-capped peaks. In the midst of this natural beauty, on the right bank ahead lay a clearing. Light reflected off metal structures—to my surprise, buildings, though I was not quite sure what I had expected. The raft landed next to its twin alongside a floating dock that extended into the river. We'd arrived at Homathko Camp.

The logging camp looked like a dilapidated army barracks held in by the seven thousand-foot slopes of Mount Evans. Four or five modular trailers, a few rusty sheds, and trucks and large machinery were strewn about in varying states of disrepair. Methodically we unloaded, hefting gear up the gangway to the shoreline. The ground was scraggly and dirt-trodden with a few low-lying shrubs and a clump

The first tent setup in the field at Homathko Camp among the sheds and machinery.

of trees a little ways away. A sandy gravel roadway led up to the trailers and sheds and continued past the cluster of trees, ending, Bryan later told us, at the air landing strip. The camp was as still as its decrepit machinery.

Stuart, Ron, and Greg had gone ahead of the others to move food boxes and gear under one of the smaller sheds to protect them from the rain portended by the overhanging clouds. Bryan nodded in satisfaction when they returned. "Have you guys seen the camp manager, Chuck?" he asked.

"No, there doesn't seem to be anybody around," Ron replied.

"Well, he knows we're coming. Let's move the rest of this gear to that shed."

It was more a lean-to than a proper shed, sheltering a small pile of wood planks. We busied ourselves moving boxes. Walking leisurely down the gravel path came a burly guy with white whiskers and a baseball hat. He didn't give a wave of acknowledgement until he was face to face with Bryan.

"Hi, are you Chuck?" Bryan inquired cheerfully, extending his hand.

Taking Bryan's hand, Chuck nodded.

"I'm Bryan," our leader said. He motioned as if to present his team. "We're the group going to climb Mount Waddington to follow in the Mundays' footsteps."

Chuck's face was expressionless. Living on the edge of the wilderness for over twenty-five years, he had surely seen every kind of adventurer. It would take more than Bryan's exuberance to impress him.

"Where can we set up camp for the night?" asked Bryan.

Chuck pointed to the field next to a large open storage shed. "You can set up there, in the field. How long you figure your trip will be?"

"If things go according to plan, we should be back here by the end of the month. We have a water taxi scheduled for August 3rd."

Chuck nodded again, his steely eyes giving no indication of what he thought about our plans.

The rain held off as each of us haphazardly tried to help get camp organized. In the open field stood a lone western hemlock flanked by a pile of aging timber. A steel-ringed firepit between the hemlock and a larger covered shed indicated this to be the designated visitors' camping spot. Surveying the shed, Bryan announced, "There's more space in this one. We should move the gear here."

Shuttling gear back and forth three or four times gave us a taste of what our coming days would be like. Finally, an enormous heap of boxes, bins, canvas sacks, and climbing equipment lay on the sandy dirt under the shelter. I didn't know how Bryan planned to organize and pack this stuff. I sat on a thick log near the shed as he orchestrated the team.

"All right, I'm going to start on dinner using that firepit in the field," he said. "Stuart, can you find the spaghetti and a tin of sauce? It's a quick and easy dinner, and we'll have time after to try to organize this lot."

With a nod, Stuart went to the cardboard boxes.

"We're going to need some wood for tent poles," Joe said. "Do you think we can use the timber piled in the field?"

"I don't see why not. We won't use it for anything but to prop the tents up," answered Bryan.

Stuart quickly found the ingredients to our evening meal, coming upon jute twine in the process. "Here, Joe, you're going to need this," he said, handing it to him.

Joe took the jute and motioned for Paddy to join him. The two men headed for the weather-beaten timber and selected between two-by-fours and thinner one-inch pieces. To build the skeletal structure of the A-frame tent, Patrick crossed two timber poles at the top and Joe lashed them together with the twine; then they did the same for the other side. A longer piece of timber secured across the top formed a ridgepole from which hung a rectangular piece of sailcloth with loops Joe had attached to the fabric. Triangular door flaps on either end, sewn along one side and fitted with button snaps on the other, would allow entry and keep out the weather. Once the two gleaming white tents were up, they looked quite handsome and livable. At least we didn't have to carry tent poles along with everything else. With an entire forest at hand, finding poles was going to be easy.

Bryan walks past the timber pile, whose wood served to prop up the A-frame tents. Photo by Greg Gransden.

At the firepit, Bryan was making a fire with matches and dry kindling he'd found by the trees. He strategically placed large rocks to balance the pot of spaghetti above the fire. The job of camp chef fell solely to Bryan, who enjoyed cooking so much that he had a side gig as a caterer. While I was fond of experimenting in my kitchen, at camp I was not as inspired. I already knew I wasn't going to fulfill the role of Phyllis in this capacity. In an archival interview she explained, "While the boys were doing most of the relaying, I was doing washing and cooking and all sorts of household chores."[3] As much of a mountaineer as she was, she was still a woman of the 1920s. I was glad we were not adhering to a historically accurate division of labour, yet it also left me searching for a task to take on. I took the metal canteens to a softly gurgling creek a hundred feet away to fill them with water. The largest one contained enough water to boil the spaghetti.

Bryan sautéed bits of summer sausage in the cast iron skillet, then emptied a can of tomato sauce over it. He heaped spaghetti and sauce onto enamel plates and we ate standing around the fire. Ron found himself a place to sit atop the timber pile. He didn't seem like his usual chatty self, bantering with Bryan, but ate quietly.

Bryan's menu plan was elaborate, with meals like beef stroganoff, Spanish rice, and lentil curry. The Mundays believed in eating well too. In the words of Don, "The notion that burned, ill-cooked food necessarily goes with camping was something we refused to accept."[4] Phyllis prepared dishes such as curried rice, boiled ham, fried potatoes, creamed carrots, and nut cake.[5] Their total bill for five hundred pounds of food reached slightly over one hundred dollars.[6]

After dinner, Bryan left each of us to choose the tasks that needed tending. I made myself useful and washed the dishes, filling a large metal pot with water from the creek and adding hot water from the kettle to warm it up. It was as simple as using a thick white bar of natural soap and a metal scrubber. With no towels or even a clean spot to set the dishes, I instinctively laid them out on the timber pile, the least dirty place available.

After dinner, the author takes to washing dishes while Patrick has an evening coffee. Photo by Greg Gransden.

The evening was still bright at 9 p.m. and we had another hour before sunset. At this time of year, the more northerly latitude of the Homathko River Valley offered one extra hour of daylight than back home. The kitchen chores done, I took a few moments to relax with a cup of tea.

"Hey, there's coffee if anyone wants," Joe announced, pointing to the blue enamel coffee pot. He poured himself a cup and found a spot between the crossbeams of the shed to lean against, took out his tin of weed, and rolled a smoke. Patrick sat by him, sipping his coffee as Bryan and Stuart went over the inventory of our gear.

I sorted out my belongings from the big communal pile. My personal gear amounted to a couple of pillowcases of clothes: a checkered wool shirt, a thin merino wool tank top, an extra pair of pants, socks and underwear. I'd been issued two pairs of 1920s-style long underwear with the button flap at the rear. Union suits, as they were called, were supposed to be worn as a base layer under other clothes. I also had a small canvas haversack from an army surplus store for easy access to essentials like my canteen, leather gloves, and blister kit.

After a long, fairly leisurely day, I started thinking about bed. With sleeping bag in hand, I headed over to the tents to claim my spot. Greg's bright red modern dome tent stood out like a map pin locating us among the forested mountains. He had already retired to his comfortable home away from home. I opened the snaps of the door flap of the closest tent and was relieved to see a canvas groundsheet laid over the grass. Since our tents were floorless and we didn't have mattresses, I'd been worried that the sleeping bags would get damp from the humid ground. Thanks to Stuart and Joe's forethought, I wouldn't have to suffer through wet nights. The Mundays, too, slept on a groundsheet, sometimes adding fir boughs as an ad hoc mattress. Air mattresses would have been a heavy and a pricey luxury that in 1926 cost $3.95 each, equivalent to sixty dollars today.[7]

The tent was barely large enough for three. Two other sleeping bags, still rolled up, were already inside. I decided to sleep in the centre, figuring I was the smallest—plus, I had a better chance of staying dry if it rained throughout the night. Sailcloth fibres expanded when wet so that water simply rolled off the surface. But a wet tent wall would release its moisture as soon as it was touched. I unfurled my sleeping bag, my fingers retracing the messages my kids had stamped in red ink on the cotton cover. I read them again and smiled. *I love you* from my eight-year-old son. *We will miss you Mom, and we all love you* from my ten-year-old daughter, decorated with heart flourishes, said it all. Even the oddly funny *Have a safe trip. Don't die* from my teenage daughter warmed my heart. All that was home, comfort, warmth, connection to my family was now my sleeping bag. It would be my reminder and my respite.

Phyllis missed her daughter Edith terribly every time she and Don went into the mountains, and always carried a photo of her pinned to her journal.[8] In 1926, little five-year-old Edith was left in the care of Jack McPhee, who lived in a cabin along Bute Inlet. Thereafter, every summer over the course of ten years, Edith was watched by friends while her parents explored the mountains. Perhaps Stuart had chosen the princess lunch box for his drone as a memento of his daughter.

As the sun set and the clouds turned to rain, Bryan and Stuart came crouching into the tent to settle in for the night. Since we had no flashlights, once the sun was down, so were we.

"There's hardly enough space for our sleeping bags," I said to them, stooping against the low ceiling of the tent. "I think if we sleep head to toe it will give us more shoulder room." I turned my bag around to sleep head to the door.

"Good idea," Stuart said.

"Aw, we'll fit all snug as a bug. I sure hope neither of you snores," Bryan teased.

This was the first time we were tenting together. It was uncomfortably cramped. There was no privacy to change, and anyhow, all my clothes were still under the shed. It was simpler to go to sleep without changing and without writing in my journal. I took off my leather oxfords and slipped them under the foot of my sleeping bag. Then I folded up my jacket to use as a pillow.

"Sleep tight, everyone," Bryan said loudly so the guys in the other tent beside us could hear.

Some grunting came in response. I could only imagine how the three broad-shouldered men were managing. Their muffled sounds soon quieted down. The patter of the rain dancing on the tent, like a soothing lullaby, lulled us to sleep.

Chapter Three

From Disarray to Chaos

THE POPPING OF DOOR SNAPS roused me from my slumber. The sun had already risen, and Bryan was crawling out of the tent. I sat up and surveyed the aftermath of our first night inside the tent. The fabric had essentially kept out the rain even though it was not waterproof by modern standards. But dark wet spots covered both Stuart's and Bryan's sleeping bags where they had been pressed against the tent walls. I felt a slight shiver and clutched my sleeping bag, pulling it closer around me. The cooler air outside wafted into the tent, bringing with it a dampness I could feel in my bones. I pulled on my jacket and buttoned the snaps. My oxfords had thankfully stayed dry under my sleeping bag. I went out to find a nice bush to relieve myself.

Clouds were floating low against the mountains and gauzy fog drifted on the waters of the Homathko. The river seemed mysterious and magical, as if about to reveal its secrets through the shifting mist. I didn't know when we'd be starting our day. The anxiety of having others wait on me was enough to break the river's spell.

I turned my attention to the shed. The food and climbing gear remained dry for the time being, strewn about under the shelter. I rummaged through my pillowcase sack to find a drawstring bag that held my toiletries: a small tin of Nivea cream, a bar of soap for washing and laundering, a washcloth and hand towel. Personal care and first aid items included nail clippers, a tension bandage, and ibuprofen tablets in case of sprains. I pulled out two essentials: a toothbrush with a tiny tube of paste and my mosquito head net. There were a few mosquitoes already flying about, and draping the net over my hat would protect me from those pesky insects.

I headed toward the firepit to find Bryan pulling a fresh pot of coffee off the fire. The warm cup chased away the shivers of the morning mist. He was preparing a feast for breakfast. In the cast iron skillet he'd scrambled a dozen fresh eggs, and was now frying plump sausages. The others were up too. Joe had strung bagels on a stick like a thick beaded necklace and was toasting them over the fire. A choice of coffee or tea rounded out this extravagant meal. I had listened to enough stories of Bryan's past trips to recognize a familiar pattern. No matter how high the mountain or difficult the hike, he always made stellar meals with whatever ingredients he had. This breakfast of fresh food was an indulgence I knew would soon give way to more basic morning meals such as oatmeal and canned baked beans.

Morning at Homathko Camp starts with building a fire to prepare the morning meal.

A hearty breakfast on the first day of hiking the Homathko River Valley. Joe uses a stick for a unique way to toast bagels.

Paddy is not his usual relaxed self this morning as he and the author have their sausage and eggs. Photo by Greg Gransden.

Patrick stood beside me with legs straddled, shifting his weight from one foot to the other and gazing vacantly at the distant mountains. He didn't seem particularly cheery today as he ate, holding his plate up high by his chest. Stuart was finishing a bagel with strawberry jam when I noticed that Ron was missing out on this feast.

Emerging from his tent, Ron was wearing the same brown shirt and brown pants as the day before. His shirt was unbuttoned, revealing his grey union suit underneath. After a night in a cramped tent, he could be excused for looking dishevelled, but his pale face and hollow eyes told a different story.

"You look like shit," said Bryan.

"Thanks, I feel like shit," Ron said, his usual soothing, velvety voice sounding rougher. He somberly accepted the hot cup of tea Bryan handed him and hunkered over his breakfast on the crossbeams of the shed.

Feeling under the weather, Ron I. takes a seat on the crossbeams of a large shed. Photo by Greg Gransden.

It was July 6, the day we would start hiking toward Mystery Mountain. So far, a day of sailing and a nice breakfast had been pretty mellow. I tingled with anticipation, preparing myself for when the tough work would begin. Unlike modern backpacking, where everything we need is contained within our packs, our expedition-style hiking would require us to ferry multiple loads a day to advance camp. In all, our gear and provisions amounted to eight hundred pounds. Food alone comprised five hundred pounds, the same as the Mundays had stocked for their five-week trek for six people.[1] Dividing our things among the six of us, we were looking at carrying three loads a day, each weighing an average of forty-five to fifty pounds. Our hobnail boots would contribute an extra five pounds to each step. To get through the valley within the two weeks we had allotted, we would need to advance a mere three kilometres a day—but with the multiple loads, this would multiply to fifteen kilometres of hiking back and forth.

It wasn't particularly early when breakfast was finished, and we still had a lot to do before we could start hiking. By 8:30 a.m. the dishes were again piled up by the wash basin. The blue enamel coffee pot sat spent of coffee. The tents were still standing. Bryan and Stuart took charge of packing while the rest of us hung around. I felt awkward, not knowing how to help, and hoped our team would soon find its rhythm. Like the evening before, I took to dishwashing and filled everyone's canteens with water from the creek. Those chores done, I turned to preparing my feet for the day's hike. I was certain that my brand new leather boots would cause blisters and hoped that with a bit of extra protection, they would not be crippling. Pulling out my blister kit, I taped my heels with a transparent dressing, then applied duct tape. Over that went a liner sock, then a wool sock, then the hobnail boots. The leather felt stiff. I stood up and lifted each foot to get a feel for their weight. The edges of the soles were studded with serrated nails for added grip. Hobnails or tricounis, invented in 1912 by a Swiss jeweller and climber, were a performance breakthrough for mountain climbers.[2] Hobnail boots were *de rigueur* for mountaineers, forestry workers, and the military until after WWII, when rubber soles became popular. Boots laced, my next task was to roll up my sleeping bag. Once that was done I was ready.

Stuart and Bryan had moved to the shed, arranging items for the first pack load. "We need the tents so we can set up camp," Bryan was saying.

"Yep," Stuart said, "I've got the saw and hatchet to cut trees for poles. The climbing gear can be left for later loads, and most of the tin cans." Bryan nodded in agreement.

"We have to move everything anyway," Joe interjected from his spot on the crossbeams, "so let's start with the tents and sleeping bags, and each of us can finish loading a pack out of what you choose to go first. We'll be done sooner and we can get going." But Bryan seemed to have his own process and dismissed Joe's suggestions. Impatiently pressing his lips together, Joe turned toward the tents, and Patrick followed after him.

I snapped photos as I waited for Bryan and Stuart to fill the packs. We had two vintage Trapper Nelson packs we'd found at an army surplus store and four replicas constructed by Ron R., a member of our climbing support team. Each pack was composed of a straight wooden frame and a large sailcloth sack fastened with a network of cordage and metal loops. Stuart's pack had been fashioned first and held eighty litres. However, with limited leftover sailcloth the last three packs were a bit smaller, holding sixty litres each.

Stuart's pack was almost full. Last to go in was his metal tool box. He pulled the flap over it and tied the pack to the

Joe helps Stuart with his pack frame as the others attempt to get the gear organized in the shed. Photo by Greg Gransden.

frame, stringing the cord through the screw eyes in a criss-cross pattern. On top of the pack went his sleeping bag. He looped the cord around it and pulled down to attach it to the frame. The assembled pack looked enormous—and only a bit of cordage remained in his hand.

Stuart answered the question in Bryan's eyes. "I think this is good for a few more packs."

Bryan blinked a few times and took a deep breath.

"Hey, I brought extra cordage," Joe offered, "though I don't know if it's enough."

In a quick gesture Bryan extended his arm to take it. "Okay, great. Let's see if it's enough. Maybe we can find some around the shed. A logging camp has got to have some."

I rolled my eyes and turned away. *Shouldn't this have been planned before?* To distract myself from negative thoughts, I left with my camera to take more shots around the camp.

It was noon by the time the six packs were tied up and ready. Joe heaved my fifty-pound pack onto my back. Immediately I felt the pull of gravity bearing on my shoulders. Don wrote in his book, *The Unknown Mountain*, "The man who cannot pack [half his body weight] all day through rough country hardly qualifies as being fully fitted to tackle the Coast Range."[3] For the Munday party, a full load generally meant sixty pounds, though Phyllis carried a few pounds less than the men.[4] Nevertheless, an impressive photo of Phyllis with a sixty-pound pack crossing Scar Creek, published in the 1927 Canadian Alpine Journal, set the bar fairly high for me.

Don Munday holding a rope tight for Phyllis as she crosses felled logs over Scar Creek carrying a sixty-pound pack, 1926. Image I-51587 courtesy of the Royal BC Museum.

Bryan and Patrick had already started toward the gravel road that led to the airstrip. I followed, filled with a mix of trepidation and relief. This is it, I thought. We're finally on our way. We rounded past the last of the rusting trucks to see the landing strip, cutting a large, open swath through the forest. The crunch of my hobnail boots on the gravel beat out an accompaniment to the sound of gathering raindrops. Joe quickly bypassed me; Ron, Stuart, and Greg were not far behind.

Stuart, Joe, Patrick, and the author walk back along the airstrip toward Homathko Camp for another load. Photo by Greg Gransden.

The wide expanse of the landing strip abruptly ended a few hundred feet ahead in what seemed like a solid wall of greenery. Bryan stopped suddenly and exclaimed, "Hey look, there's a bear." Ahead of us, a small black cub briefly made an appearance, then ran off to find its mother in the bushes—the same bushes we were about to enter.

Ron took this moment to readjust his straps, Stuart helping him with the massive pack. Stuffed to capacity, they were not comfortable. The unpadded straps dug into my shoulders painfully, and I could already feel them beginning to bruise. I told myself encouragingly, it's just a bruise, ignore it, you'll be fine. It wouldn't have bothered Phyllis, who seemed to me indestructible and rather stoic. Since her mid-twenties she suffered from arthritis in her knees; she claimed it was only "a bit of a nuisance" when in fact it caused her so much pain, she often applied cool compresses to reduce the swelling, and even had trouble sleeping.[5]

Radiating down one arm was a new tingling sensation. The strap was cutting off my circulation. As pack strap material, I was discovering, sailcloth had been the worst choice because as it was pulled taught, it rolled in on itself like a rope. I paused to take out my leather gloves from my haversack and wedged them under the strap to cushion my shoulder, but to no avail. The fingers on my left hand would tingle for hours.

Patrick bent over to relieve the weight from his shoulders. "Oh mother!" he cursed. He tucked his own gloves under one strap and his felt hat under the other. He seemed to be having the same painful problem. Coming from a strong, burly guy, it was reassuring to know it wasn't only me who was suffering. These were tough guys. I needed to be tough to prove I wasn't the weakest link. I couldn't show fear, uncertainty, weakness, or pain: I had to remain as stoic as Phyllis was. Whatever discomfort I was experiencing I quickly put out of mind with my mantra: *just keep going, just keep going*.

Once we got to the end of the landing strip, the faint trail of an overgrown logging road could be seen. One by one we entered, Bryan leading with Ron behind him, then Stuart and Joe, Patrick and I, and finally Greg bringing up the rear. Leaving the open space of the landing strip and stepping through the forest barrier was like taking in a breath before diving into water. From now on we were in an entirely new environment. The logging road was less a road than a maze. The trees on either side grew inward, reaching to close the gaps between them. Small bushes reached upward to fill the centre space. I could only see ten to fifteen feet ahead of me before the foliage obscured my view. Whatever creatures lurked behind the green veil we could not see. The sky itself was barely detectable. The intensifying patter of rain bounced off the leaves of the trees that enveloped us. My world shrunk to my feet stepping in front of me and my ongoing mantra.

A further twenty-five minutes down the trail, I heard Joe cursing loudly and looked up to see his pack hanging awkwardly off-kilter from his shoulders. The strap had ripped right off the frame under the weight he was carrying. We all stopped. Joe slid the broken pack off and it landed on the muddy ground with a thud. He shook his head. "I knew this was going to happen," he said.

Stuart put down his own pack and pulled out his metal tool box to devise a temporary fix. As we waited, Bryan took out his pipe. He seemed to have confidence in Stuart's repair skills. "Are we having fun yet?" he asked rhetorically. Burdened like pack mules under the rain, we were too engrossed in our own discomfort to reply. "I guess this shows us how well these packs are going to hold up," he added blithely. A puff of smoke floated away.

Starting down the overgrown logging road with Patrick, the author carries an enormous pack. Photo by Greg Gransden..

Joe looked up from the busted pack. "Maybe we should lighten the loads a bit?" he suggested.

"Ah, we'll all be used to this in a few days," Bryan said with a cocky grin. He tapped his pipe and put it away. "Stuart, see what you can do with the pack. I'm going to continue on with the others."

Hunched over the pack, Stuart glanced sideways. A muddy trail in the rain was not the best of conditions to sort out what went wrong and fix it.

A few minutes later, we found Bryan kneeling in the mud beside his own pack. His strap had also ripped off the frame. With two broken packs, there was no way we could go much further, nor ferry the three requisite loads that day. It was already early afternoon and we had barely hiked two kilometres. The day was not going well. Doubts about the viability of this expedition filtered through my mind.

Bryan was forced to reassess. "We'll make camp here," he hastily declared. We dropped our packs in the middle of the overgrown logging trail.

It was not an ideal spot to camp. The trail was waterlogged and narrow, and we'd have to line up our tents in a tight row. The rain and mud exacerbated the urgency of setting up camp. There was a lot of work to be done, and amidst the chaos, I was still unsure of how to contribute. Bryan began hacking at the bushes with his machete to clear more space for the tents. Stuart pulled out his handsaw to cut thin-trunked trees for tent poles. Joe searched for stones to encircle the firepit, and Patrick rummaged for dry wood for kindling. I helped Stuart set up the tents and lay down the groundsheets, and chucked the sleeping bags inside to keep them dry. Bryan started sorting through the food to find the ingredients for the beef stew he was preparing for our evening meal. In what seemed like an attempt to show he had control of the situation, he told Stuart, Joe, Patrick, and I to take the four unbroken packs and go back to Homathko Camp to bring more loads. It was mid-afternoon and we still had plenty of daylight left. Having already sighted a bear, he told us, "Don't forget, we're in bear country. I want everyone to stay in pairs." Grabbing empty packs, Stuart and Joe started hiking back together. Patrick and I picked up the other two and followed.

Paddy, with saw in hand, consults Stuart on setting up camp in the middle of the bushy trail.

For the next three hours we marched back and forth between the two camps. Unburdened, the way back to the starting point was an easy forty-five minute walk. But when I was loaded down by a heavy pack, my mind was unable to engage in any conversation and I went into something like a trance. The trees were a blur of green, the soggy dirt path guiding my feet. The pain radiating from my shoulders subsumed the annoyance of the mosquitoes who managed to slip under my head net.

Eventually the rain let up. On a more relaxed walk toward Homathko Camp, Patrick told me, "I really can't see how we're going to make it with these packs. They hurt like hell and they're falling apart."

"Yeah," I said sympathetically. I was demoralized too but trying to convince myself we could overcome this hurdle.

"This is not going to work. Bryan really should have figured this out way before," Patrick continued in a slightly higher-pitched voice. "What's he going to do now?"

"I guess he'll have to figure something out," I said. Questions churned in my head. *What if we can't repair the packs? What does this mean for the expedition? How can we carry on?* We lapsed back into silence, the rhythmic sounds of our boot steps calming my nervous thoughts.

On our final return to camp at around six that evening, Bryan's large pot of bubbling stew was ready. Patrick and I added the last load of the day to the mound of provisions that we'd set at the far edge of camp lest we have any animal visitors. The food was feebly protected with a brown tarp flung over the pile. A backpack containing the most aromatic meats was strung from a tree to keep it out of reach of bears.

"Come and get it," Bryan announced, picking up the ladle.

I scooped a ladleful of stew into my bowl and ate standing up. Each mouthful was warming and hearty and somewhat made up for the miserable day. The rain and incessant mosquitoes had intensified the physical demands of an already tough hike. My hat and jacket had kept my top half dry, but my rain-soaked knickerbockers stuck wretchedly to my skin. There was no point in changing into my only other pair of pants to get them wet and muddy too. I moved closer to the fire, rotating front to back like a rotisserie and coaxing the heat from the flames to dry my legs.

To eat, I had to lift my head net over the brim of my hat, exposing more skin to unending swarms of mosquitoes who feasted on my temples, forehead, neck, and hands. Without the strain of hauling loads to distract me, it was almost unbearable. I willed my body to ignore the itching and ate quickly so I could pull my head net back down and put on my leather gloves. We were not allowed to use chemical bug repellant because Bryan insisted on historical accuracy. Joe brought out a couple of litres of a concoction he'd cooked up with citronella and other natural oils. He tested it by rubbing the juice onto his skin.

"Is it working?" Paddy asked, looking hopeful.

"Ahh, maybe," Joe said, holding out his exposed arm for the experiment. Soon he was slapping off winged paratroopers. "For about a minute it works. I think it's too diluted. I probably should have cooked it longer to concentrate it."

I let out a disappointed sigh. There seemed to be no respite. I wanted to escape to my sleeping bag. Milling about the fire, our faces obscured by head nets, we looked like mournful lost souls in a scene from WWI. The waning light desaturated the greenery of the forest, blending the layers of leaves into a uniform charcoal grey deepening to black. Humidity infused every inch of the forest and the dank earth released its decomposing aroma. The dark mud remained slick and wet and stuck to our boots, and we unanimously named this place Mud Camp. We dropped our empty cans into the fire to burn off the food smells and added them to the trash bag that we carried with us. Leftover bits of food we buried in the rich earth.

The tent I crawled into at bedtime was even more crowded with our personal belongings stuffed inside, edging out a space at our feet or under our heads as pillows. It had been such a trying day, I couldn't be bothered to brush my teeth or write in my journal, preferring sleep's escape. Again, I kept my clothes on, only taking off my knickers to lay them on top of my bag. Cocooned in my sleeping bag, my body finally relaxed and my mind wandered.

Our first day on foot had begun in disarray and quickly turned to chaos. The fact that we'd taken so long to get our packs together that morning was evidence that our food storage and transportation systems were not fully thought out. It had worried me that I didn't know how Bryan planned to organize the food, but I'd trusted that he would plan adequately with enough waxed cotton sacks.

I'd expected the packs to be heavy and was prepared to tough it out, and I'd anticipated blisters from my new boots. The mosquitoes I hadn't considered would be quite so bad, and bears were an ever-present concern. But it wasn't the brutal loads that slowed us down, nor the physical discomforts, nor the rain and mud. We had made one grave error. As outdoor adventurers we should have known to trail-test our gear before we headed into the wilderness. We had no idea how well our handmade packs, tents, and sleeping bags would perform under harsh conditions.

The Mundays were far better prepared. Phyllis and Don had spent a decade field-testing their equipment prior to their 1926 expedition, and spent their winters preparing for the climbing season, repairing packs and gear, and waterproofing their clothing and tent.[6] Phyllis was in charge of planning menus and dehydrating foods, and made careful estimations of quantities to avoid superfluous packaging.[7]

Before setting out for Mystery Mountain, the Munday party also made reconnaissance trips, scouting routes and leaving caches of provisions along the way. Local logger and trapper Jack McPhee, who lived halfway up Bute Inlet, took Don Munday and Johnnie Johnson on a preliminary excursion four kilometres up the Homathko River by motorboat. Don and Johnnie soon returned with the aim of getting most of the team's supplies as far up the Homathko as possible, depositing equipment and provisions at fur trappers' shelters situated along the riverbank, roughly where the Homathko intersected with the Heakamie and Jewakwa Rivers.[8] Trapper Patchell's cabin was eleven kilometres up the Homathko, and August Schnarr's cabin sat a further thirteen kilometres away.

During the 1926 expedition, Johnnie and Athol canoed further supplies up the river once the use of their gas boat became unnavigable after Patchell's cabin. Don, Phyllis, Bert, and Thomas hiked on foot to reach Schnarr's cabin as far as the Brew Creek tributary to move forward their provisions.[9] Despite the Mundays' advance planning, it required dogged determination and enormous effort to reach the glacier in thirteen days. Even the Mundays hadn't anticipated how long it would take to relay supplies in the Homathko River Valley. Never had Phyllis and Don encountered such an unwelcoming territory.[10]

Expedition-style backpacking required a Munday level of organization to be as proficient as they were. But these cabins no longer existed, and even though canoes might have sped up a few kilometres of our progress, overall it would have been impractical and far too dangerous. More important, the seven of us hadn't had the opportunity to venture into the valley together before now, partly because we hailed from different cities. Patrick lived in Calgary; Bryan, Ron, and Joe in Toronto; Stuart in Ottawa; and Greg and I in Montreal. And Bryan had focused so much on dressing and gearing up like the Mundays, had been so seduced by his romantic notion of explorers, that he'd overlooked how harsh the wilderness could be. Relying on your gear as if your life depended on it was essential, because it did.

Chapter Four

On a Thin Line

THE NEXT MORNING, the daylight seemed dull through the tent walls. Bryan and Stuart had already awoken and left the tent, leaving me luxuriously alone. I could hear the clang of metal against rock, maybe the coffee pot, and shuffling movements outside my tent. Throwing off my damp sleeping bag, I checked the state of my heels, pulling back the tape I'd slept in. The blistered skin was soft and pruney, as if I'd sat in a bath overnight. Skin in such a delicate state was prone to infection. I made a mental note to remove the tape every evening to let the skin breathe. To prepare for another day of hiking, I applied a new dressing and more tape, then pulled on two pairs of socks and the usual knickers and puttees—still slightly damp, but I hoped my body heat would help them dry out.

I exited the tent with my toothbrush and paste and canteen in hand. My personal grooming was as simple as brushing my teeth. Another morning ritual was a visit to the latrine a hundred feet from camp. I walked down the trail until I saw the ice axe planted into the ground, the pick end holding a roll of toilet paper. Next to the axe, a hole dug into the forest floor served as our facilities.

Back at camp, Bryan was standing by the mound of provisions, hands on hips, head shaking at what Ron was saying: "It's been one day, and everything has gone wrong. We should go back to Homathko Camp, regroup, and fix the gear."

"No. If we turn back now, it'll be harder to get going," Bryan replied.

"At some point we'll be so far out that we can't turn back." Ron gestured to add weight to his words. "I don't think any one of us wants to be stranded because we didn't take care of things now."

Bryan was adamant. "No. I'm not going back. We don't lose one inch of ground."

Raising his arms in a shrug, Ron let it go. Arguing didn't seem to deter Bryan from his plans. We accepted that he was the leader of this expedition, yet I sensed that he was trying hard to be decisive and in control. Without seeking input from the team, he announced the day's program. Stuart and Joe would remain at Mud Camp to repair the defective packs. Greg would also stay behind to get footage of their work. The rest of us would carry on to the next camp.

After oatmeal and bacon for breakfast, Bryan, Patrick, and Ron prepared for the hike the way Joe had first suggested at Homathko Camp: we each loaded an empty pack with our sleeping bag and personal effects, then filled the remaining space with cans, food, and communal gear that Bryan had sorted out for the next camp. We would choose a new site depending on the time of day and the suitability of the area.

While we were getting our packs ready, Greg sent a message with our GPS coordinates to our field coordinator, Renee. For the most part he was staying out of the re-enactors' way and filming from the periphery. He didn't have the same packing challenges but did have his own share of weight to carry. In addition to his camp gear, climbing harness, and mountaineering boots, his large modern backpack carried camera equipment, a portable solar battery charger, four industrial-size batteries for backup, a water filter, and the satellite communication device.

Once we were good to go, Bryan led the way down the overgrown logging road with Ron behind him, then Patrick and I. The weather had cleared up and I was glad to leave the muddy camp and get moving. I focused on getting into a rhythm: breath, step, mantra. *Just keep going.* Raspberry bushes tempted us from the edges of the path, decorated like Christmas trees with bright red berries. At points along the trail I lost sight of Patrick ahead of me, then eventually found the guys resting while waiting for me. I didn't pause, but kept going at a pace I knew I could sustain for the whole day, hoping to gain some ground before they caught up to me again. My eyes cast downward at the packed dirt, I noticed a large heap of bear scat full of berry seeds at the side of the trail. With so many ripe berries around, bears were definitely in the area. The hair on the back of my neck stood up at the thought and I resolved to stay within eyesight of the guys.

Time seemed to disintegrate during the hike that morning. It was one tree after another, a bush, a patch of grass again and again. Hunched forward from my load, I noticed the trail becoming more sandy. The trees thinned a bit, opening to more sky, and I heard a faint rush of water. My pace perked up in anticipation.

Ahead of me Bryan called out, "Over here, we can cross over here."

The old logging road dropped off into a ravine, where it was washed out by sand and rocks and a small river bringing meltwater down from the mountains. In midsummer it was at its lowest point, but we still needed to cross it. I saw the nearby twenty-foot log extending over the edges of the ravine. Beaming, Bryan said, "This will be our Munday crossing."

We'd all seen the photo of fearless Phyllis crossing felled trees over the much more torrential Scar Creek. Unlike the Mundays, we would not be cutting down trees for river bridges.

The author crosses a log over a small stream. Photo by Greg Gransden.

Tree felling was dangerous enough without aiming the trunk to land precisely across each edge of a precipice. I imagined myself as Phyllis navigating her way across the abyss. This little gully was plenty wide enough for me. The log was at least eighteen inches wide and solid, the river rippling ten feet below it. When it was my turn to cross, I stepped cautiously onto the log, unsure of my balance with the bulky pack and heavy boots. Slowly I inched my way across, my hobnail boots' toothy edges gripping the bark and securing my footing.

Safely on the other side, we wound our way through low-lying bushes and downed logs to come upon a sandy clearing. The sand was soft and white and gleamed in the bright sunshine. A stream ran the length of the clearing and formed small pools before descending into the ravine, giving the area a beachy feel. Beyond lay a panorama of mountains with a high waterfall cascading down a rock face from the hidden glaciers above.

"This looks like a perfect spot to camp," declared Bryan.

We dropped our packs in agreement. Compared to Mud Camp, it was spacious, clean, and dry. Ron headed to the stream and knelt down to dip his canteen in the cool, clear water. We emptied our packs into a heap and Bryan and I draped our sleeping bags over a bush to let them dry in the sunshine.

But there was no time to waste. We had more loads to bring. Retracing our steps over the log bridge, we trooped back along the logging road.

At Mud Camp, Stuart had sacrificed a section of his canvas groundsheet for the new pack straps. He and Joe had cut strips off with a knife and hand-stitched them to the packs with twine and a sewing awl from Stuart's tool box.

"That's great work," Bryan exclaimed, clearly relieved to see the repairs complete. "Let's have a quick lunch before we take the tents down and hike another load. There's bagels, cheese, and sausage."

The new pack straps were thicker and stiffer than the sailcloth, and though unpadded, felt like they were in comparison. Nevertheless, my shoulders ached on those tedious hikes back and forth. I started mentally measuring distances between camps. An internal voice floating up to my consciousness in waves tried to convince me that physical pain was only a sensation.

That afternoon at the sandy clearing, the work of setting up camp began. Leaning over the provisions to pick the ingredients for the evening meal, Bryan looked up at me to say, "There's one more load to bring. Can you go with Stu, Joe, and Patrick?" I gazed at him unblinkingly. "Please," he added. I didn't feel like hiking another two hours, but nodded in acceptance.

Stuart hangs a tent on the ridgepole.

By the end of that day's six-hour haul, I was exhausted and filthy. The sun had brought warmer temperatures to the valley and dried up the trail. The back of my hiking shirt, pressed against the pack frame, was bathed in sweat. Once I'd dropped my last load, I headed straight for the pools near the stream and dipped my red cotton bandana in the water to wash the grime off my face. While Bryan cooked dinner, I settled myself on some smooth round rocks and soaked my tired feet in the cool water. Hopefully, the problems of the day before were finally behind us. I was looking forward to a meal and a relaxing cup of tea.

Refreshed from my poolside cleaning, I changed my denim shirt for my woollen one. Mosquitoes were coming out to haunt the early evening air, and a thicker shirt afforded more protection along with the head net. I sat down on the sand to join the guys around the firepit. The campfire was quickly becoming the hub and heart of the social arena, where we ate and drank and relaxed after a long day. Bryan was a permanent fixture at the fire, cooking or smoking his pipe. Today he'd prepared pasta with bits of ham he'd salvaged from the smoked hocks that were starting to go mouldy in the damp weather.

With bellies full, we were able to decompress and reflect on our situation. The discussion quickly homed in on the fact that the trip was not going well. Having the packs break so early was either the result of a design flaw, an indication that we were overloading them, or both. Without Stuart and his tool box, such extensive repairs would not have been possible. The first two days had also demonstrated the extent of time and energy it took to move multiple loads only to advance camp a few kilometres. If we could reduce the number of loads of food and gear, we could cover more ground. Deciding what to leave behind was up for debate.

"We're taking too much food in," said Bryan. "Some food we can leave for the way back, so why carry it with us?"

"Yes, absolutely," said Joe, leaning back against a large rock and rolling a joint.

"We can trim the extra stuff we don't need, like canned fruit and evaporated milk. The cans are the heaviest," Bryan went on.

Joe shook his head. "No."

"What I'm saying is we leave the cans," Bryan clarified, making a crossing-out motion. "We don't take them."

Joe shifted his weight to one leg and glanced downward before taking a fortifying breath, as if preparing for battle. "We need the canned food. It's the only food that's going to make it to the glacier," he said emphatically, pointing up the valley.

Bryan didn't seem to understand Joe's point. Our food storage system was essentially to pile provisions on the ground. While the cans were impermeable, the cured meats and dry foods had only cotton sacks—not all of them waxed—and a tarp to protect them from animal raids and weather. It was not an ideal system. After a day and a half of rain some foods, like the ham hocks and summer sausage, had already begun to show spoilage.

Patrick, Stuart, and I watched the exchange without making any remarks. Ron sat slumped on a rock, pouring himself tea and quietly drinking it. No one seemed to take any notice of Greg circling around us, filming Bryan and Joe reiterating their viewpoints until they came to a common understanding. We would recalculate how much food we needed and take most of the cans with us, and we'd leave caches of extra provisions along the way to claim on our return trip.

The author's 1921 Kodak camera shows a glimpse of camp life at the second campsite: Bryan sits by the campfire and Ron I. heads for the tent.

We soon found that the clouds of mosquitoes were even more horrendous here than at Mud Camp. Having marked a plentiful source of fresh blood, they'd brought in reinforcements. Unable to gain entry through my head net, they feasted on my exposed hands holding my cup of tea. Itchy red welts formed. The smoke from the campfire dissuaded some of the attackers, but I had had enough and decided to escape to my sleeping bag. Inside the tent I realized there was no escape. Waiting under the apex of the tent's white walls were dozens of thirsty beasts.

Even after I'd snapped the door shut, the mosquitoes found entry between the snaps and under the sides of the floorless tent. Quickly, I changed into my one-piece union suit to sleep in. Pulling up my sleeping bag as much as I could, I wrote half a page in my journal. Then I switched out my brimmed hat for an army surplus toque—not because it was cold, but for added protection under my head net while I slept.

It didn't rain overnight, but it was uncomfortable and damp inside the cocoon of a down sleeping bag designed for chillier conditions. A few times I awoke, my body covered in sweat. I wanted to throw open the bag and release the buildup of heat, but I knew the bloodthirsty mosquitoes would dive-bomb me the moment I did. I shifted around and tried to go back to sleep.

Morning came on the third day with more bright sunshine. I opened my eyes to see the ceiling of the tent completely blanketed with mosquitoes. They must have been attracted to the carbon dioxide the three of us had been exhaling through the night. This camp was spectacular but it had a dark underside. I penned the name Mosquito Camp in my journal.

Before breakfast I decided to try out my 1921 Kodak and photograph the camp from across the ravine. Soon I'd be taking shots of the glaciers' shimmering walls of ice, tiny specks of men climbing along their ridges. I couldn't wait to capture, like Phyllis, the grandeur and beauty of the mountains.

I crossed the log bridge, more confidently now, and found a vantage point that encompassed the camp and the surrounding mountains. I expanded the accordion-like bellows of the camera and held it at waist level, looking down into the small viewing glass to compose the shot. A soft click accompanied the pressing of the shutter. The mechanical simplicity of this camera was quite elegant, powered only by levers and a crank knob to advance the film. I was drawn to this little camera much like I was drawn to the expedition itself: both were scaled down to their essential forms. Each required less reliance on technology and more on creativity and skill. True, feather-light, compact hiking equipment and feature-rich digital cameras solved certain problems, but they also allowed a lapse in rudimentary abilities such as bushcraft and survival techniques, or the basics of light exposure on film. To me, this 1926-style expedition was a reclamation of fundamental skills that we had lost in modern society.

As captured by the author's 1921 Kodak camera: Mosquito Camp at the edge of the ravine.

Back at the firepit, we gathered around a breakfast of oatmeal. The discussion we'd started at dinner the night before was getting underway again when Bryan interrupted with an announcement.

"There's another concern. Ron isn't feeling any better."

Ron was on a rock, hunched over in an almost fetal position. He looked weak and lethargic and had been deteriorating over the last couple of days.

"Yeah, I don't want to go but this bloody flu is not getting any better," Ron said, his face forlorn. "I can't go further into the bush. It's just not safe."

"Patrick has told me his blisters are a problem," Bryan continued. "He can't keep going at this rate. So I'm hiking them both back to Homathko Camp today."

The camp fell silent. Grimness and sadness were palatable in the air as we absorbed the news. It was a significant blow to our team's morale. We were losing two of our biggest and strongest guys, a full third of the crew. The expedition had reached a tipping point. We were on a thin line between being fearless adventurers braving adversity and fools who didn't know when to stop.

But the expedition was Bryan's passion project. He firmed his chin in a show of resolve.

"We've got Mark and Ron R. meeting us at the glacier in about a week. We've had a slow start, but with the fixed packs and trimming down to the essentials, it might take a few extra days but I'm hoping we can make it."

"We need a better plan than that," Joe interjected.

"Yeah, of course. We'll look at what we have and figure out a plan," Bryan replied.

"It's already eight," Joe said. "We should have figured this out last night. We're on day three and I don't even know what we're doing today. We can't keep dragging on days like this." He paced back and forth, looking agitated. I sensed his confidence in Bryan's leadership was wavering. "We have to do something or we're never going to make it."

Mustering up some energy, Ron lifted his head up at Joe. "Bryan just said we're going to look at the whole thing and figure out a plan. He didn't say he had decided a plan, he said we're going to figure out a plan."

Joe gave a dismissive scowl. "Yeah well, we have to change the strategy."

Having to adjust to another setback was, I thought, not as great of a problem as the discord brewing among our teammates. My preference would have been to put our heads together rather than the chest-beating display I had just observed. But the loud, somewhat aggressive discussion inhibited me. An introvert by nature, I felt more at ease speaking to people individually. After Bryan had left the campfire, I cornered him by the tent.

"Bryan, the team is about to fall apart. As the leader you have to rally the troops. Give us a bigger goal to focus on."

A sheepish expression crossed his face. "I'm trying. It would help if everyone were on board." He went off to help Ron prepare his pack for the hike back.

I had noticed Patrick's lighthearted humour fading as quickly as his doubts about the expedition grew. His smile had left him soon after we arrived at Homathko Camp. It was only later, after the expedition that he confided that personal life stressors had magnified the challenges we faced, leaving him unable to deal with so much uncertainty. It had made him uneasy to see key preparations being done the day before our departure, and he was anxious not knowing how our food would be secured along the trail. I empathized with him on the painful packs and boots and the unforgiving environment. Ron's departure was his only chance to pull out.

I said my goodbyes with a hug. "Feel better," I said to Ron, reaching up around his tall frame. His dream of climbing Mount Waddington with Bryan was lost.

Bryan left the remaining expedition members with one request. "While I'm gone, can you each go through your gear and whittle down what you need to take with you to the bare essentials?"

The three of them set off over the log bridge and disappeared into the forest. Bryan wouldn't be back before early afternoon.

The warm sun beaming down over Mosquito Camp restored our spot to a beach oasis. The leaves of the pale-barked red alder trees dappled the sunlight as we sat under their shade. The tall, slender trees, typical in wet and recently cleared land, could have easily been mistaken for birches, though it was lichens that were responsible for the whitish colour of their bark. The clear pools by the creek were perfectly sized for bathing, though not very private. Smooth white rocks lining the pools invited us to come and take a dip. There was no way of knowing when the next bathing or laundering opportunity would present itself. I decided to wash away the grime of the last few days, using my underwear as a bathing suit since Greg was filming. The water was cold but not icy. I washed my hair and hiking clothes and hung them to dry in the sunshine. Greg, Stuart, and Joe took their turns in the pools and relaxed on the surrounding rocks.

My next task was to pare down my personal belongings. I hadn't packed excessively to begin with, and I'd have to make do with even less for the next twenty-six days. For the sweaty work of hiking I designated one shirt, one sports bra, one pair of pants, two pairs of socks, and the puttee leg wraps. For camp, I packed my leather oxfords plus extra socks, the merino wool tank top, and underwear; for sleeping, the union suit. I didn't know what Phyllis used as a brassiere, considering that our modern bra wasn't widely in production until the 1930s. She may have had a bandeau bra that looked much like a tank top. For colder weather on the glacier, I packed my wool check shirt and sweater. Essentials to protect against rain, sun, and thorny devil's club included my rain jacket, hat, red silk scarf, and leather gloves. My camera bag, film, journal, toiletries, and blister kit I wouldn't part with. That left an extra-thick sweater, a shirt, pants, and sunglasses to stuff in a pillowcase sack and leave behind.

In terms of group gear, Stuart was certain to bring the hatchet, saw, and tool kit. Our climbing equipment was heavy but essential for glacier travel. Leaving behind two ice axes and iron crampons didn't save us much on weight. The ineffectual bug juice Joe had made was certain to remain at Mosquito Camp.

Stuart's tool box was an essential piece of equipment.

The team's vintage mountaineering gear included wooden-stemmed ice axes and hemp rope.

When Bryan returned, he got Stuart to help him sort out what food to take and what to leave behind. The sixty-pound bag of flour would be needed for making bannock, biscuits, and pancakes. The bacon and summer sausage provided necessary protein and calories. A selection of canned corned beef, beans, and sardines would also come along. Extra items such as condensed milk, soy sauce, pastas, and chocolate bars we could make do without. I noticed the wrappers on the cans were starting to disintegrate from the wet weather and the stress of loading and unloading into packs.

"Hey Greg," I called out, "do you have a marker or something I can write with on the cans?"

"Actually, I do. I have a Sharpie. Hold on a sec." He headed to his tent and handed me the marker. With a little detective work, I identified the contents of the cans so we wouldn't be surprised to find condensed milk instead of beans for dinner further down the trail.

By the time we'd worked out the logistics, it was too late in the afternoon to start ferrying loads forward. Another day was lost. The distressing events of the morning were still simmering in my mind. What did Ron and Patrick's exit mean for the expedition? The difficulties of the past two days had understandably unnerved us all. Bryan seemed overwhelmed, and rather than acknowledge the tension or inspire us with tales of the Mundays' bravery and resilience, he focused on cooking our evening meal of salt cod with fried potatoes and creamed carrots.

Gathered around the campfire that evening, it wasn't long before Joe was on his feet, presenting his concerns like an orator to his audience. "It's been a lovely day here, but it also means we didn't get anywhere," he said. It was the end of the third day and we had not advanced more than five kilometres from our starting point. "We have fifty kilometres of valley to get through and no idea how much bushwhacking there will be." He pursed his lips. "We need a jump start. Get up earlier, hike longer, go harder."

"Sure, Joe, we will," Bryan said.

Joe ignored this. "We could have moved some loads ahead or scouted, done something today. At this pace, there's no way we're going to make it," he said, gesturing up the valley toward Mount Waddington.

Stuart, Greg, and I listened as Joe continued with his rant and Bryan offered weak explanations. "We needed to fix the packs," he said. "Ron was sick."

"This is not working." Joe paced around the campfire. "We need to change our strategy."

"How, Joe?" Bryan said finally, sounding exasperated.

Joe shrugged his shoulders. "I don't know. How about gaining some ground every day? I know I could hike five kilometres right now and be back before nightfall."

"We need to stick together," Bryan countered.

"We'll never make it," Joe insisted, shaking his head.

This last jab seemed to hit a nerve. Bryan' voice rose from frustration to real anger. "What would you do, Joe?"

They were going round and round on the same point as if stuck in a loop, getting no further along. Their combativeness was incomprehensible to me. Bryan was reacting to Joe's criticisms rather than diffusing the argument and opening the floor to the team members. Each of us had our own motivations for joining the team, and in the face of challenges, we'd need to take into account our differing objectives in deciding on our course of action. Bryan was missing this entirely. I believed we had to be in it together or not at all. If we shared our personal goals, if we got to know each other better, perhaps Bryan could draw on this information to build more cohesiveness in the group. His leadership would not be diminished, I thought, if he actively sought out others' opinions and advice. This would demonstrate how he valued each person for their contributions. Stuart's skills were evident in field repairs. I was struggling to feel useful beyond being a pack mule.

But I didn't mention any of this, immobilized by the volatile environment. It wasn't a safe forum to open up in. In the heat of the discussion, Stuart and Greg also remained quiet. Joe overpowered the discourse.

After most of us had dispersed, Bryan remained at the firepit, staring into the flames and seemingly absorbed in thought. I retreated to my tent to write in my journal. In it I was free to gripe and whine and ruminate to my heart's content. I complained about being uncomfortable and itchy and how terribly rough the terrain was—only to find it worse the next day. I felt like a fifth wheel, disconnected from the guys. There was an inner conflict I couldn't pinpoint. I worried about whether I was strong enough, if I could keep up on the trail. And I was keenly aware that my failure to speak up was tied to a lack of confidence. Anyhow, were I more outspoken as Joe was, I wasn't sure how it would be received. If Joe were a woman, I suspected that the other guys would dismiss his emotional outbursts as being hysterical.

That second evening at Mosquito Camp, the entire fate of the expedition hung in the balance. I didn't know at the time that Greg had taken Bryan aside to express his misgivings about the trek and his desire to call it quits. Bryan confided this close call to me a few days later when we were alone in the tent. He recounted the story with his usual expressive gestures. “I was frantic,” he said, his eyes wide. “I had to find a way to convince him to stay or we were done.” The film Greg was producing was a key feature of our fundraising efforts, and our sponsors were counting on it.

“What did you tell him?” I asked.

“I said to him, stick it out another day and if you’re still unhappy and don’t think the film will work, I’ll walk you out myself.” A sly smile crossed his face. “Then the next day I said the same thing.”

In preparing for this expedition, I thought, curled up in my sleeping bag, we’d all focused on the gear and the weight and toughing it out. We wanted to learn what made the Mundays so resilient by mimicking their demanding route and their equipment. But by this point it was clear that simply dressing in 1920s clothes and bearing heavy packs through overgrown bear-tracked bush would not make us resilient. The grit and determination we needed to face what the Homathko River Valley had in store for us required much more than physical toughness and a gung-ho, push-through-it attitude. The valley was not going to reveal its secrets or its lessons so easily. Like schoolchildren on their first day at school, we were bewildered and struggling to adjust.

Chapter Five

Tears and Fears

I WOKE IN THE TENT ALONE. Bryan was up early, brewing coffee by the smell of it. It was a lot roomier now that Stuart had moved into Joe's tent. I aired out my sleeping bag to freshen it up, shaking out Bryan's too in thanks for his cooking. There was no further discussion as we ate our oatmeal. We seemed to have assimilated the events of the past two days. We went about the tasks of dismantling camp. Greg washed dishes as the rest of us packed, his bright blue backpack ready to go. The plan for the day, July 9, was to move camp in multiple loads to the next suitable site we could find.

Before leaving Mosquito Camp, we chose a spot next to some low-lying bushes to pile up the extra food and personal possessions to be left behind. A brown tarp was thrown over the mound and weighted down at the corners with rocks. I had packed extra clothing as security against being cold and wet. Stripping down my personal effects to the bare necessities lightened my load, but also left me feeling psychologically vulnerable. It felt as if I were going into the wilderness with just the clothes on my back.

When confronted with challenging situations, we all gravitate to soothing behaviours, our own personal safety blankets. After a long day or an argument with Joe, Bryan seemed most relaxed preparing meals by the campfire. Stuart worked with his hands, making repairs, cutting poles for tents, and once, carving a wooden spoon. I noticed Greg, usually at mealtimes, asking Bryan about the day's plan, how far we'd hiked, where we were on the map. Perhaps the idea of being lost, even temporarily, was unacceptable to him. Joe's volatility dissipated when he was having his cup of coffee and rolling his weed.

My haven was in the tent with my sleeping bag. It was the place I felt the cleanest and most relaxed. After a day of hiking I'd wipe the grime off myself and change out of my dirty, sweaty shirt. I obsessed over remaining healthy and uninjured. The wooden pack frame was bruising the back of my arms, and the strap was irritating the skin on my left shoulder. I didn't rely on the group's first aid kit, preferring to use my own supplies. Even though my blisters were under control, I continued to tape my heels every morning and removed the dressings every night to air them out.

Without time wasted on debates, the five of us were able to get ready quickly and start hiking. The old logging road, which had ended on the other side of the ravine, picked up again past the sandy campsite and headed northwest. I was glad to be moving. Waiting around at camp with the ever-present mosquitoes was uncomfortable. Hiking distracted me from the itchy bites, and anxious thoughts couldn't linger in my mind as we penetrated deeper into the valley.

The overgrown logging road continued unendingly. From Bryan's map we surmised that the trail ran parallel to the Homathko River, though it was impossible to see the water—or much of anything besides trees. Tall alders lined the way, their flittering leaves rustling in a breeze that didn't quite reach us. Sunshine beamed down from above, making for another warm day and chasing away the mosquitoes. I could finally take off my head net.

After an hour of plodding along and playing catch-up with Bryan and Greg, overtaking them and then falling behind again, the road ended abruptly. We'd come to the edge of a precipice. Directly in front of us, fifty kilometres up the valley, was our first glimpse of the Waddington Range. Some twenty peaks gleamed in the distance, blanketed in snow. Mount Waddington looked impossibly far away. Even though it was the tallest peak entirely within BC, from this vantage point it was dwarfed by the nearer mountains rising steeply on either side of the river.

I wasn't in a great rush to climb the icy slopes that lay beyond. Glacial terrain posed objective hazards, and though I felt confident enough on moderate inclines, I didn't fully trust our hemp rope and iron crampons. I had already decided to opt out of climbing Waddington if I felt the danger was too great.

Joe and Stuart were peering down into the void by their feet, where the Homathko River flowed below. "Oh man, look at that," Joe exclaimed. "This is a dead end."

Bryan came up behind them. "The road is supposed to go straight through but there's nothing but the river," he said, perplexed.

"See there," said Stuart, sweeping his finger in a wide semicircle, "the river must have changed course, swooped around, and washed the road out."

The Homathko swelled with glacial meltwater every spring, and the sediment it carried accumulated into shifting islands that forced the water to go around, digging out new channels. This arm of the Homathko looked more like a lake than a river, at least one kilometre wide and stretching out just as far in the distance before us. The tree-lined shore formed a dark green band against the cloudy green-grey water.

The logging road comes to an abrupt end at the washout where it had been claimed by the Homathko River. Joe and Stuart pose with a first glimpse of Mount Waddington in the distance. Photo by Greg Gransden.

"The road must continue on the other side," Bryan said thoughtfully. "We'll just have to go around."

He went crashing into the woods, scrambling up the hillside to find a way around the washout. One by one we followed him, balancing over fallen trees and digging into loose soil to come up to a ridge. Hiking off-trail was immeasurably more difficult with the uneven footing and bulky packs snagging on branches. The air was rich with the sweet odour of Douglas fir, and the light was muted under the canopy of the tall conifers. We followed the ridge on what looked like an animal trail. Paths like these, created by racoons, deer, bears, and cougars treading the same route over and over again, were often the easiest way through an area. Bryan followed the wisdom of the animals along the ridge until the trail flattened out and connected back to the logging road.

Trooping down the human-made road was less inspiring than our detour through the bush had been. The forest in its natural state was like a secret garden teeming with a lush diversity of plant and animal life that lived in harmony, filling me with wonder.

We hiked for another hour, cloistered by alders that yearned to reclaim the path for their own. Sweat saturated my shirt and the red silk scarf around my neck. Forging ahead of me, Greg pushed aside slender branches that rebounded to whip me in the face, arms, and legs. I dropped back to let him widen his lead and to avoid further slaps. Eventually, Bryan stopped at a small clearing and dropped his pack.

"We should camp here," he said confidently to Joe and Stuart behind him.

On the left side of the trail stood a tall, thirty-foot-wide rock wall. It seemed to have been erected to prevent river waters from eroding the logging road. To our right, the trees were held back by a massive rocky outcrop. It looked as if chair-sized grey-black boulders had tumbled down the mountain and come to rest. Bryan was eyeing a slab that jutted out from the outcrop to form a natural platform at hip height. "I can put the campfire on this flat rock. It would make an ideal standing stove," he said, patting the hard surface.

A rock wall erected by loggers to keep the swells of the Homathko River from washing out the road.

The boulders beckoned with their large, flat faces to climb up and see what lay on the horizon. For hours I had felt the still, hot air of the forest, caged in by wiry branches. I heaved off my pack and clambered up the rocks to be greeted by a panoramic view of the Homathko River flowing below snow-capped mountains that hugged its western shores. Standing on the rock pile, I drew in glacier-cooled air and released the tension from my shoulders. The expansiveness of the river and mountains liberated me. It was almost as if I could touch the sky, even the sun. Though this jumble of boulders was nowhere near the elevation of a mountain, for a brief moment, I closed my eyes and imagined that I was on top of the world. This sense of freedom, of seeing the land laid out before me, was what I was here to experience. With its glorious vista of the valley, I decided to name this place Mountainview Camp.

We spent the day hiking back and forth five times between Mountainview Camp and Mosquito Camp. Had we made such good progress from the beginning, we might have been almost halfway through the valley by now. It felt good to have completed such a productive day. Perhaps our troubles were behind us. Stuart and Joe set up the tents and I tried to help by holding up the poles. Greg went to fetch water at a stream not too far away, and Bryan prepared Spanish rice for dinner.

Bryan prepares a meal at the standing stove at Mountainview Camp.

We gathered around the hearth and ate well, buoyed by good spirits. We had hiked a good distance—but we were still behind where we wanted to be on the map.

"How far do you think we hiked today?" Greg asked, looking to Bryan.

Joe took this as a general question. "I think we covered maybe five kilometres."

"I don't know," said Bryan. "It seems to me we made good progress." He pored over his topographical map, trying to estimate our position from the features of the landscape. As would-be 1926 explorers, route-finding was limited to a paper map, a compass, our own sense of direction, and keen observation of the terrain. When Bryan had planned the route, climbers who knew the area had advised him to stay on the logging roads because they led to three key bridges that were the only way to cross wide, treacherous rivers and get through the valley. Though Bryan's map showed contour lines of elevation, it didn't indicate the location of the roads or the bridges.

Bryan stuffed tobacco into his pipe and settled back on a rock, looking relaxed as he smoked. I sipped my tea. Joe paused his chatter for a puff of his joint, then raised his hand in offering. "Stu, you want to try?"

"Hmm, sure, okay," Stuart said in his usual even tone, accepting the joint.

I half listened to the guys' banter, which to my ears seemed like a game of one-upmanship for the worst experience, or funniest or strangest. Greg joined us around the fire, encouraged by the somewhat fewer mosquitoes. I noticed his head net was a bit too short and didn't quite cover his neck.

Despite being able to escape to his bug-free tent and sleep on a cushy air mattress, he was experiencing the rough trail as much as the rest of us.

As dusk fell over camp and we headed for bed, so began our nightly battle with the mosquitoes. A friendly rivalry sparked up between the two tents. Joe and Stuart swore their Armour Up technique worked best. Rather than sweat it out in their sleeping bags, they slept fully clothed from head to toe in their thickest wool sweaters, socks, and hats, plus bug nets and gloves, providing armour against the mosquitoes.

Bryan and I used the more refined Smoke 'Em Out technique. Starting with an empty tin can, we put in dry moss and a hot coal to create smoke. Placed inside the tent by the door, the smoke would fill the tent and eliminate almost all the bugs. As Bryan and I settled in for the night, we'd kill or remove the stragglers and use duct tape to seal the gaps between the door snaps. Our boots and clothes we pushed up by the tent sides to prevent the bugs from gaining access under the door flaps. I could finally sleep without a head net and without sweating buckets in my sleeping bag. If there could be any luxury in the valley, it was a mosquito-free tent. There was only one important caveat: there were to be no night runs to the loo.

Another sunny morning greeted us on July 10. During our preparations for the day, Greg came up to Bryan to show him a map he had stored on his phone. Before the expedition Greg had consulted with filmmaker Bradford McArthur, who, two years prior, had followed the Arc'teryx team of professional athletes on their attempt to re-create the Mundays' route to Mount Waddington. McArthur had shared his map with Greg, drawing the locations of the bridges relative to the rivers, the sections on the logging roads, and areas of bushwhacking off-trail. According to this map, we could follow the logging road until we reached the first bridge over the Heakamie River. I was glad Greg had had the foresight to capture the map on his phone. In the thick of the valley, staying on route might not be obvious.

This time it was Stuart who led the way out of Mountainview Camp, taking us down the logging road with long, solid strides. Greg went next, then Bryan and Joe, and I brought up the rear. Though roughly delineated and narrow, the hard-packed dirt road was easy to follow—at first. Not far along, the road seemed to disappear, overtaken by a section of fast-growing boxelder maples. Their disheveled-looking leafy branches reached over ten feet high, swallowing the sky and making it harder to navigate. No longer could I make out the trail ahead of me. All I could see was Joe's hat bobbing through the swaying bushes. Since Ron and Patrick had left us and doubts about our preparedness had entered my mind, I'd begun mentally mapping the terrain, thinking that if I needed to retreat I could make my way back to Homathko Camp on my own. In this tangled bush my apprehension grew at the idea of being alone; I was not sure I could find my way back. I resolved to stay close to the bobbing head before me.

Joe suddenly froze and I stopped behind him. Obscured by the bushes, Stuart's soft, quiet voice ahead of us said, "Greg, hand me your bear spray."

Greg must have obliged. He was the one carrying the group's two cans of bear spray since they were modern gear.

My senses jumped into a heightened state of awareness. My skin tingling, I listened intently.

"Hey, bear. Hey, bear," came Stuart's placid voice again.

I stood immobilized, waiting for something to happen. After what seemed like longer than a few seconds, the faint, muffled sounds of cracking branches and the relaxing of Joe's stance ahead of me signalled that the incident was over. We caught up to Stuart, who sounded calm as he told us how he had stepped through the bush to come upon a large grizzly bear crossing through a creek bed. He and the bear, surprised to see the other, had exchanged a look for a brief moment before the bear ran off into the woods. Stuart let out a long breath and put away the bear spray, this time into his own haversack. We continued along our way, keeping to the safer side of the creek bed.

Every bear encounter has the potential to be dangerous. The Mundays had a number of close calls. On one occasion, a grizzly pounded up to Don and stood roaring at him, so close he could feel its hot breath.[1] Don noted in *The Unknown Mountain*, "Phyl, believing the bear meant to leap down on me, typically enough, charged the roaring brute with an ice axe."[2] He never mentioned how terrifying such encounters were for her.[3] I just hoped the bears stayed far enough away. I was not certain I could live up to the mythology of fearless Phyllis.

The bushy thicket began to thin out, giving me a peek of clear skies, and soon a clearing opened up around a large marshy area. It was a quintessential jammed-up beaver pond, the water dark and murky. We skirted around the shoreline through short grass and over downed logs. As we tramped back through the trees, the ground remained soft and muddy, rivulets of water trickling around slippery rocks. We clambered up and down small gullies, hanging onto trees for support as we wound our way forward.

We'd made good progress on the hard-packed dirt logging road, but navigating through the bush was painfully slow. My pack was loaded to capacity, and each time I shifted my weight it pulled me off balance. I took out an ice axe to use as a short walking stick, but still I struggled to adjust to the rough terrain. My hobnail boots' serrated edges caught on a log and I tumbled to the ground. Propping myself up with the shaft of the axe, I wobbled back to my feet. Slightly shaken, I tried to step more carefully as we trudged through groves of tall trees, Stuart leading much of the way. But I tripped over a root and fell a second time. What the hell, I thought, surprised that it had happened again. Then a deep dread descended upon me. This was the easy trail. *What am I going to do when it gets steeper and harder?*

An important lesson I had learned from a woman mountaineering instructor years ago was to examine why mishaps occur. My foot had slipped on a climb up a snowy slope, and I'd slid down the incline before being caught by my safety rope. Needless to say, falling is not recommended on a mountainside. In riskier situations we need to understand how our mindset and physical body affect our actions. Falls are generally the result of fatigue, inattention, or lack of skill. Right now, in the middle of the Homathko River Valley, I knew it couldn't be fatigue as I was nowhere near my physical limit. I told myself to pay attention.

I treaded even more cautiously, sloshing through rivulets, stepping over decaying logs with dry branches sticking out like crooked dead bones. The marshy forest was like an obstacle course. Then my foot was pulled out from under me and I was falling again—keenly aware, this time I experienced the fall in slow motion, the weight of my pack pulling me sideways and my hands grasping through air for something to latch onto. And I was down in a rivulet. My body had betrayed me again. Joe was behind me and helped me right myself with my pack. Panic was beginning to set in. *What if I can't do this?* The thought echoed through my brain. Through my self-absorption I vaguely heard Joe's voice saying, "These packs are too heavy and unstable. She could have impaled herself."

Over the course of the three-hour hike I tripped and fell four times. Each fall was another blow to my confidence, sending shock waves of alarm through my mind. The same questions looped over and over: *How will I make it on vertical terrain? What will happen to the team if I bail?*

Reaching a grassy clearing, Bryan paused and called out, "We can leave our loads here and pick them up tomorrow." The clearing wouldn't work as a campsite but we'd hiked long enough, and the spot would be easy to find again when we came back this way. I dropped my pack like a sack of potatoes and took a long drink from my canteen, trying to swallow down the guilt and blame constricting my throat. We emptied our packs of their contents and retraced our steps toward Mountainview Camp. Familiarity did not breed confidence. I took no notice of the trail, of the boneyard logs and rivulets we were crossing once again. Instead I withdrew into myself, ruminating on the chilling realization that falling was failing. I feared the steep terrain we were soon to be up against: Scar Mountain, with its tall dark conifer trees clawing at me with angry branches. The earth would disintegrate beneath my feet and pull me down, leaving me to fall further behind.

With empty packs, we made it back to Mountainview Camp in two hours. I retreated to my tent to wipe off the grime of the day's hike and change into cleaner clothes. Then I sank down onto my sleeping bag and stared blankly at the tent ceiling, trying to process my feelings. I felt as if I had a weight on my chest, pinning me down. For days I'd been mired in trepidation; at some point it would be revealed that I was not the ideal Phyllis Munday. I was not as fearless, or as stoic or as strong. The last six months of daily workouts and strength training at the gym hadn't served me well that day. I'd stumbled, not once but four times, a sure sign of weakness. In a group of men that revered being tough and sucking it up in the face of hardship, I worried about being *the girl.*

When dinner was ready, I took my bowl of pasta and joined Bryan atop the rockpile overlooking the Homathko River. I stabbed at the noodles, not really in the mood to eat. I needed to get this heavy feeling off my chest and the only way was to say something, but what, I did not know.

I dragged in a breath and choked out, "Bryan, I'm worried about myself. I'm not sure I can do this."

As the words left my mouth, it was as if a pressure valve was released, and so too were my tears. I tried to maintain my composure but couldn't entirely keep it from spilling out. Down by the campfire, Greg must have seen the unfolding drama and quickly emerged on top of the rocks with his camera.

I was emotionally exposed but tried to ignore his presence. Releasing the truth was more important than holding back my tears.

Surprised, Bryan put his bowl down. "What do you mean? You're doing great."

"No. Today was horrible and we're still on easy terrain. I don't want to slow everyone down because I can't go as fast or as long," I explained, my voice quavering.

"But you didn't slow anyone down," he said empathetically.

"I'm already giving my all. How do you know I can do it when it gets harder?"

"I know you can do it."

But his consoling words couldn't register in my brain.

After dinner, I retired to my tent to write in my journal and reflect on the day, relieved that I'd released that great buildup of emotions, at least. My head was clearer now. Though I hadn't known when or how it would happen, at some point I knew I would hit my anxiety wall. Now that I had, it was up to me to decide if it was going to stop me from continuing on.

I asked myself what was really holding me back. I was not hurt; I could still hike. I had everything I needed: food, shelter, health, the safety of the team. Even if it didn't feel like it, I was getting stronger every day, tromping around in my five-pound hobnail boots. And then it dawned on me: falling a few times did not mean I had failed. I just needed to learn to walk differently in those hobnail boots. Instead of my usual small steps, I needed to really lift my feet and take big, wide steps like the guys did. And come to think of it, though I could carry as much weight as they did, it stood to reason that my pack weight be proportional to my petite frame. Now that I realized it, there was nothing physically holding me back other than the anxieties in my mind.

Besides, I had worked so hard, dedicated all my energy to be part of this expedition. I had sacrificed time with my family and other projects to work on the website, write newsletters and sponsorship proposals, attend fundraising events. I had spent hours and hours researching the Mundays and the period they lived in. It seemed absurd to give up because I'd tripped a few times.

Phyllis Munday serves meals at camp, 1926. Left to Right: *Thomas Ingram, Athol Agur, Phyllis Munday, Don Munday, Bert Munday, and Johnnie Johnson. Image I-68083 courtesy of the Royal BC Museum.*

It was quite possible that I had made Phyllis into an unattainable superhero figure. Naturally, I felt pale in comparison. Putting aside Phyllis the mountaineer, Phyllis the anomaly who was stronger than a man, I considered Phyllis as a wife, a mother, a woman. She thought about her daughter Edith in the weeks she spent away from her in the mountains. She suffered from arthritic knees. She dutifully served meals and cleaned camp as any housewife did in the 1920s. She was an ordinary woman made extraordinary by her skills, her strength of character, and the freedom she felt in the mountains.

My horrible day had only been horrible because my underlying fears of not being capable had revealed themselves. I needed to quiet my inner critic harping on who I was supposed to be and just be a woman, here to experience the wilderness. I was determined to continue on despite the uncertainty each day would bring. My thoughts grew fuzzy, my tired muscles relaxed, and I drifted off to sleep.

Chapter Six

The Murky Middle

I AWOKE THE NEXT MORNING feeling lighter in spirit and open to letting the valley reveal itself. Leaving a few non-essential victuals behind, we carried another load from Mountainview Camp over the same boggy obstacle course that had caused me such despair the day before. With a renewed mindset, the trail now felt perfectly ordinary in a wilderness adventure kind of way. With the adjustments to my stride and pack weight, I didn't fall once.

Over the next few days we settled into a more orderly routine, still starting off in late morning but making steady progress on the old logging road. Bryan cooked at the campfire; Joe chopped firewood; Greg and I fetched water and washed dishes; Stuart fixed and mended. Frustrations and disagreements dissipated and we finally seemed to find our rhythm as a team.

I greeted each day with the intention to be fully present and to set aside critical self-doubts. In the process I became more curious, more in tune with my surroundings, and I began to relax into new roles. In this group, I now understood, tasks need not be given but could be chosen. At our next camp, I felt empowered enough to pick up the machete and chop small trees into tent poles. From Stuart, I learned different ways to stack kindling to make a fire and how to use rocks to retain heat. At another camp I volunteered to dig the latrine, a chore that Joe usually took on. Planting the ice axe to mark the spot, I hung the toilet roll on the pick end with satisfaction.

The author gets into her stride. Flanked by Joe and Stuart at Fernbed Camp. Photo by Greg Gransden.

Now that I saw Phyllis in a new light, as a woman who also felt fear, discomfort, and pain, I was likewise shedding my expectations for myself and becoming conscious of a deeper facet of my identity. I called her my inner wild woman, who resides in the depths of my soul and arises in awareness of my body. This part of me knew that I needed to release the fearful emotions hindering me on the trail. I found myself relating to the valley with a deeper level of reverence akin to the Mundays, who had profound respect for the forests, rivers, and glaciers they discovered. Don's experience of the mountain wilderness was ineffable. "There is a great deal more than mere pride in priority to pioneering," he wrote. "The first pilgrims to invade the immemorial silence of gleaming aisles of guarded sanctuaries in the very essence of things know feelings even they cannot recapture when they revisit those scenes."[1]

A blue enamel pot of cowboy coffee is always on the fire.

After a day of adventuring was done, Joe always had a pot of cowboy coffee brewing over the fire and invited us to gather for a cup. This ritual was our time to relax and socialize. Without any filters, we'd wait for the grounds to settle before pouring, but a few grains always made it into our cups. Although I didn't usually drink coffee, especially not black, grainy coffee, I came to look forward to the coffee part of the day.

The relative ease of following the logging road helped us advance a good three to five kilometres each day. But we had already seen where sections of road disappeared into the bush, slowing us down significantly.

"Maybe we can scout ahead," Joe suggested, checking on the blue enamel coffee pot. "I can wake up early and check it out. That way we won't be in for any surprises."

"Okay, Joe, if you want to do that, or maybe you and Stu," Bryan replied.

His tone with Joe had changed since our frantic first few days, listening more, directing less. He'd realized the value of Joe's ideas, and in turn, Joe was complaining and arguing less. Scouting provided Bryan with important information about what lay ahead and gave Joe an important leadership task.

On the evening of July 12 at Rockslide Camp, I found Bryan sitting by the fire, studying his topographical map under his vintage reading spectacles. I looked over his shoulder at the map.

"I think we might be here at this corner," he said, pointing to tight-set contour lines that represented a steeply rising ridge. Bryan knew from Greg's hand-drawn map that the route to the bridges would take us on a detour about five kilometres eastward to glacial tributaries that fed their waters into the Homathko. "We've been heading east. We must be close to the Heakamie," he surmised. "We might hit it tomorrow."

The Heakamie bridge was the first of the three key bridges we needed to cross to get through the valley. Our next goal would be to find that bridge.

Bryan finishes bathing in the waterfall pool, where the air is blissfully cool.

By the middle of the following day, we'd hefted two loads from Rockslide Camp about three kilometres forward, but still the bridge remained elusive. We carried one more load, continuing a bit further down the logging road in hopes of reaching it. The brilliant sun had heated up the valley, making it feel tropical. Bryan, Stuart, and Joe had stripped off their shirts, revealing sweat-soaked union suits underneath. Sweat dripped off my nose. We were hot and tired and in need of a break. The road led up a gently sloping incline bordered by alders and maples. I noticed a cool breeze wafting by me, almost like air conditioning. Then came the sound of burbling water. A little ways down from the road, a stream cascaded into a deep pool of water surrounded by flat rocks. The timing was perfect, as if the valley knew we needed a waterfall oasis. We shed our packs and ran to frolic in the cool water, peeling off our clothes and washing away the sweat and grime. After we finished bathing, Joe got out to make a fire in the middle of the trail and start some coffee. Bryan had brought a lunch of bagels with summer sausage and cheese, and we ate leisurely, revelling in our natural air conditioner.

Relaxed and invigorated, we decided to scout some more and track down the Heakamie bridge. "Before we come to the bridge, the trail splits in two. We have to take the fork on the right," Bryan informed us.

We followed the road—and then it vanished at a clearing at foot of a hill. It was a dead end. Letting down his pack on a patch of scraggly grass, Bryan scanned the area, weighing his options.

"It looks like there might be a trail going up the right side of the hill," he said, running a hand through his hair and scratching his head. "I'm going to take a look."

"I'd like to come with you," Greg said, grabbing his camera.

"Okay. We shouldn't be too long."

The rest of us disburdened ourselves and waited half an hour, seeking shade from the hot sun under a clump of scruffy shrubs. Bryan and Greg returned to report that they'd found nothing but dense bush.

"Why don't we split up and scout in different directions?" Joe proposed.

"Makes sense," Bryan said. "I really want to find that bridge. We must be so close."

Joe, Greg, and I teamed up and followed a possible path up the hillside, scouring the ground for a way back to the logging road. Scouting felt different than hiking. Unencumbered by a heavy pack, I was the exhilarated to find out what lay around the next bush. This feeling of perpetual discovery must have been a large part of what motivated the Mundays to explore the wilderness.

We found no hint of the road, though, and Stuart and Bryan also came up empty. We regrouped at the grassy patch at the bottom of the hill and took a drink of water. It was already 4 p.m. and getting late in the day to keep looking. Bryan was baffled at the road's apparent disappearance. He set his jaw and gazed intently at the surrounding trees and the texture of the ground to find a clue for his next decision. He shuffled around the edges of the clearing and stopped to examine a pile of downed trees more closely.

"Hang on, there might be something here," he announced.

The heap of trunks was hiding a faint gap amidst a tangle of bushes. It wasn't obviously a path, but left with no other option, Bryan felt it merited investigating. I joined him and Greg in scouting the area.

Soon enough the gap widened into a definite path, and after an hour of hiking the bushes thinned out, indicating newer growth. Then we heard the low roar of rushing water. Bryan in the lead let out a jubilant "Whoo-hoo-hoo!" that echoed through the valley.

There was the bridge over the Heakamie River, its waters rushing violently through a narrow canyon. In joy and relief we raised our hands to give each other high-fives of victory. It was a typical concrete bridge with metal guardrails, built for road traffic and looking absurdly out of place in the middle of nowhere. I couldn't quite figure out how loggers' trucks had made it out this far. There must have been other connecting roads that had since been swallowed by the proliferating vegetation.

The concrete base and metal railings of the Heakamie bridge seem incongruous in the middle of the forest.

The Heakamie River surges through a canyon under the bridge.

We regrouped with Stuart and Joe and returned to Rockslide Camp. It had taken all day—a full nine hours of trekking—but we'd found the first bridge. And now we had a firm landmark to place us on the map.

After an easy dinner of baked beans and cured bacon we gathered around the fire. Bryan, Stuart, and Joe sat on the packed dirt ground and I found myself a rock to perch on. Greg remained standing, fidgeting with his phone.

Bryan put down his paper map. "The Heakamie bridge puts us at about halfway through the valley," he noted.

"And it's taken over a week to get there," Greg ventured. It was evident to everyone that Bryan's plan to hike the valley in ten days was unrealistic. It was already the end of our eighth day on the trail. Greg slid his phone into his pocket and kept his hands sheltered inside. "How long is it going to take us for the next half?"

"That's only because we lost three days at the beginning," put in Joe, who always had something to say. "If you're so worried about time, we can get started earlier and cover more distance."

Greg didn't look convinced. "Even if we make it to the mountain, I'm just not sure we'll have enough time to hike back through the valley."

"We have a few days of leeway," Bryan said. "I know I said we could get through the valley in ten days, but I planned for two weeks in, a week on the mountain, and two weeks back out."

I wondered if Bryan was being idealistic again. Before it had been his friend Ron's pragmatism that kept his optimism in check. Now Greg was stepping into this role. He pulled out his phone again, brow furrowed, and showed us his map.

"Up to now we've been on the logging trail. After the next bridge there won't be a road. It's full-on bushwhacking and a horrendous bog."

"I don't know, I expect that's what we're here for. No one said it was going to be easy," Joe said disparagingly. He took a short puff of his joint. "Besides, we'll have less weight to carry so it'll probably take half the time."

"There is no way hiking back through this forest will be that much faster. There is just no way." Greg tilted his head. "I really don't want to hike through this again. I think we should fly out."

"Yes," I said, nodding. "I don't want to go through this bush again."

"Then what's the point of doing it Munday style?" said Joe, shaking his head.

For the Mundays, being flown out of the valley had not been an option. With ten kilometres of mountainous glacier travel to cover and only four days of rations left, Don concluded, "Of course we would make an attempt to reach Mystery Mountain."[2] Perhaps the Munday party was made of sterner stuff. In an epic thirty-one hour grind they reached Mount Waddington, pushing themselves to extremes of fatigue and hunger.[3] I certainly did not want to push that hard. The valley was proving to be challenging enough.

Bryan mulled over Greg's idea. If we no longer needed to reserve two weeks for the hike back, we'd have more time to get through the valley and climb the mountain. For this reason he and Stuart were both in favour of being flown out. Joe seemed disappointed that we were willing to compromise on historical authenticity, but as he was outnumbered he reluctantly acquiesced. Bryan asked Greg to send a message with his satellite device to our field coordinator to work on a helicopter pickup.

On the next day, we easily passed the Heakamie bridge and continued down the old logging road. Under my pack strap, the irritation around my left armpit and shoulder was getting worse, but there was nothing to do but keep marching on. The familiar, plodding rhythm of our days was lightened by the high notes of Bryan singing a lively ditty before they were absorbed by the forest. The sun shone down brightly on the thickets of alder trees lining the trail, the leaves danced, and I caught myself humming along.

The Jewakwa River parts the curtain of forest to reveal a stunning view of the mountains beyond.

We didn't know we were nearing the next bridge until we'd stepped on it. Like the Heakamie, the Jewakwa bridge was built of concrete with metal side rails, but covered in patches of lichen and moss. Below the bridge the Jewakwa river ran flat and wide, cutting an opening through the forest to reveal triangular-shaped mountains in the distance. The sun was low enough behind the mountains to cast a shadow over the river. Views such as the one before me were hard to come by in the depths of the valley, and I paused to take photos. When we left the bridge we were once again enveloped by the forest.

The trail rounded down a slope and flattened out into a clearing. A few scraggly bushes clung to the earth but the land was mostly open and flat. Given the late time of day, Bryan decided it was a good spot to camp. Jewakwa Camp was nestled in the kilometre expanse between the rising foothills of Landmark Mountain and the swiftly flowing Jewakwa River. After setting up camp and dinner of rice and beans, Bryan drew our attention to his plan for the next day.

"We've made good progress the last few days," he said, sitting cross-legged with pipe in hand. "Tomorrow we have a big day."

I listened attentively as I sipped my tea, preparing myself mentally for the slog ahead. I'd need to make sure to pack enough water and a bag of nuts for energy.

"McArthur's map shows that from here on in, the road ends and we'll be bushwhacking through a murky middle part until we get to the big bend in the Homathko River," Bryan explained. The big bend, as the Mundays called it, was where the river took a right-angled turn around the spur of Landmark Mountain. "The next section is a long stretch through a bog. According to the notes on the map, we can keep to higher ground and do some sidehilling to avoid it."

Greg looked for a reaction from Joe or Stuart, and when none came he asked, "Where do you think we'll make camp next?"

"I don't know. We'll have to see how far we get."

As I was getting ready for bed that night, I felt a dull pain on my shoulder. I reached behind me to feel a large raised bubble on my skin. *What the hell is that?* I thought. Half undressed in my sports bra, I came out of the tent to ask the guys to check it for me.

"We have to pop the blister," Stuart said, examining my shoulder. He got out the first aid kit, and I flinched when I saw the needle in his hand. As expertly as he had repaired the packs, he fixed and bandaged me up.

The next morning, July 15, we packed our loads and walked the remaining stretch of logging road. Roads in the bush, we discovered, were not always continuous. Some sections connected to other roads and others seemingly dropped off into nothingness. When our road ended, a trail unfurled through a patch of Douglas firs, wide and cleared of brush. Tied to the tree branches were bits of bright pink tape. We had entered an area that surveyors had flagged for a new road, possibly as far back as a decade ago when a private hydroelectric dam had been proposed for the valley.

Like Hansel and Gretel following bread crumbs, we followed the flagging tape through the dense, dark forest, looking for flashes of neon pink among the foliage. Thick bushes and ferns obscured the targets of our scavenger hunt. Offshoots from the main trail branched off in every direction, making it hard to keep track of which was the centreline. We wandered over the deep brown forest floor, going left, then right, then backtracking when the tape came to an end. Bryan and Stuart didn't seem too worried about our meanderings, though, and I figured they would eventually find the way. We knew we had to go southwest first, then head northwest to contour the foothills of Landmark Mountain. If we veered too far to the right we'd run into the mountain; too far to the left and we'd eventually hit the Homathko River.

"I think we're getting off course," said Joe, who had a keen sense of direction. "This trail is taking us eastward."

"We're following the flags," Bryan said, taking off his hat to scratch his head. He turned in a circle and scanned the trees.

Greg approached Bryan rather stiffly, holding his satellite device. "Bryan, this doesn't make any sense. Why don't I use the compass on the SPOT device to check for the right direction?"

We hadn't intended to use the device for this purpose—only for essential and emergency communications. Evidently, Greg felt that the situation warranted a compromise in our approach. But Bryan didn't answer, just kept puzzling over the landscape, trying to glimpse a flash of tape. Greg turned on the device and stared at the compass on the screen rotating as he turned, stopped, and turned again, trying to get his bearings.

Joe shifted his feet. "Look, we're wasting time again. We need to go west, so let's just go west."

"That's what I'm trying to figure out," Greg said with an edge in his voice. Joe shot him a reproachful look.

Bryan set off through the trees again, his brow creased in concentration. Eventually he hit upon a piece of tape that marked the centreline of the proposed road and confirmed our direction. On it was written *Jewakwa* with an arrow pointing one way; another arrow pointed toward the Homathko River.

We had been hiking for a few hours and lost precious time trying to find our way. We happened upon a clearing that marked a brief interlude from the canopy of the trees, a good spot to leave a cache. I was happy to sit down on the short, grubby grass and take a break. I had a swig of water and popped a few nuts in my mouth before passing the bag around. Then we emptied the cans out of our packs and hiked back to Jewakwa Camp.

After a dinner of corned beef hash, we sprawled around the campfire, tired out after a long day. Stuart picked up Bryan's map and studied it.

"We were fine heading southwest, then we must have continued too far rather than turn northwest to follow the contour line," Stuart guessed.

"The way through the valley is fairly straightforward," Joe said with a sour expression. "I think we're still wasting a lot of time." He looked pointedly at Greg.

Ignoring Joe's obvious dig, Greg turned to Stuart and Bryan and asked, "How far do you think we got today?"

"Well, it's hard to tell," Bryan said slowly. "We probably didn't make as much distance as we would have liked."

"No, of course not," Greg grumbled. "We didn't even know where we were exactly. How can we keep moving if we don't know where we are?"

Joe picked up his coffee and set it back down, twiddling with the cup, his face screwed up as if trying to hold back. Then he burst out, "There is no fuckin' way we're going to make it to the glacier at this pace. This is insane." He glanced sideways at

Greg. "I don't know why we aren't getting up earlier. We could easily put in a couple more hours every day. Something has to change. Maybe we can have our packs ready the night before. I came here to climb a mountain, not slog through a bush."

"It takes me five minutes to get ready," Greg said curtly. "My pack is ready to go and my tent comes down fast."

Greg didn't mention that his sleeping problems had him waking after eight in the morning. On the other hand, as the team's filmmaker he wasn't expected to take on the time-consuming camp chores.

Bryan didn't intervene, having learned that Joe needed to vent his thoughts. Joe repeated himself until he gave up on his monologue and sat staring glumly into the fire.

When the team was getting along and feeling good, it seemed that no obstacle could slow us down—even if we did start hiking at ten or eleven in the morning, quite late compared to the Mundays, who considered 7 a.m. to be a delayed start.[4] But arguments and disputes impeded our progress and impacted our mental resilience in dealing with the challenges of the valley. And now, the positive momentum we had enjoyed as a team was starting to slip. Greg, who had been silent on much of the earlier debates, was becoming more vocal about our plans. I suppose he was realizing that any situation we found ourselves in would also affect him, re-enactor or not. I thought him prudent to ask about distances and camp locations. But it was clear that his sense of security was under a lot of strain in not knowing precisely where we were on the map. The idea of getting temporarily lost in the woods didn't bother me as much, provided that I stayed within the safety of the group. With Greg's satellite communication device, I knew we were one message away from a helicopter ride back to civilization.

Greg's cautiousness was causing Joe obvious frustration. For Joe, the GPS and helicopter pickup went against the nature of the expedition. Our mission was to remain as historically authentic as possible to gain a full experience of what it had been like for the Mundays. But the feasibility of this mission depended on how much risk each of us was willing to tolerate. We were already being pushed to the limits of our comfort zones. It was impossible to know if using Greg's modern technology would diminish our re-enactment experience or save us from disaster.

Chapter Seven

Unspoken Bonds

I HAD TO CATCH MY BREATH and be still for a moment to take in the extraordinary scenery that surrounded me. Tall Douglas firs stood sentinel in the sloped cathedral of the old-growth forest, soaring two hundred feet high, their trunks at least six feet wide. Under lofty western hemlocks, frothy woodland ferns dappled the landscape with soothing green tones. Light filtered through the high canopy and settled on the forest floor, a rich brown carpet of dry needles that muffled the sound of our footsteps.

We'd started that morning from Jewakwa Camp, this time easily navigating through the surveyors' paths and past the cache we'd left in the clearing to reach this breathtaking grove by midday. I could smell the earthy decay as we walked around the exposed roots of a fallen tree. The energy radiating within this forest was very different from the confinement I had felt on the bushy, overgrown logging road. Perhaps these century-old giants held memories of the Mundays as they explored the valley.

Bryan passes through an old-growth forest. Photo by Greg Gransden.

Stuart and Joe led the way, following an animal trail along the sloping ridge of the forest. Greg hiked behind them in the centre of our pack, with Bryan and I at the tail end. The air was still and humid under the hot sun, and when we came across a trickle of glacial water sprinkling down a rocky outcrop, we gratefully stopped to refill our canteens. For much of the next three hours we were sidehilling across the ridge, the awkward angle causing much discomfort in our ankles. I was careful to point my downhill foot slightly outward for better balance, reducing the likelihood of spraining my ankle.

Minor accidents and injuries are an ordinary part of mountaineering. Don and Phyllis Munday experienced their share of incidents as they spent their lives exploring mountains together, ten of those years in the Waddington Range.

Some incidents could have been avoided, such as when their companion Athol Agur drank river water before it settled properly and developed stomach sickness.[1] Glacial rivers are milky with sediment, carrying finely ground rock flour milled by the shifting glaciers. Other afflictions were harder to foresee. As the Munday party crossed a glacier near Mount Waddington, the glare of the snow intensified the ultraviolet rays of the sun; Phyllis wasn't wearing her glacier goggles and became snow-blind, a condition akin to sunburn of the cornea. Though she could barely see she carried on to the next camp, led by the hand by Thomas Ingram. For days, her eyes were extremely sensitive to light and felt like sandpaper. Tea poultices helped to ease the pain.[2]

Not all dangers could be eliminated; objective hazards that formed part of the environment, such as rockfalls or bad weather, were always a risk. Don's newspaper and journal articles told of escaping avalanches, huddling together in terrible thunderstorms, and managing dangerous river crossings.[3] The Mundays also encountered forty-acre log jams, swamps of red slime, and rising flood water.[4]

Neither Don nor Phyllis would have been able to accomplish their impressive mountaineering feats without the other. From their first meeting in 1919 at an outing with the British Columbia Mountaineering Club, they discovered that they shared an unspoken bond. Climbing up the loose rocks of a glacial moraine, Don lost his footing and Phyllis instinctively jumped under him to break his fall into a steep gully.[5] In future explorations, Don depended on Phyllis to lead climbs when his left arm, permanently weakened by an injury at Passchendaele in WWI, became fatigued and could no

Don and Phyllis Munday pose at Seymour Creek near Grouse Mountain, BC, sometime between 1920 and 1928. Image I-61772 courtesy of the Royal BC Museum.

longer grip.[6] Don wrote of their relationship: "We had stood together undismayed by the appraising eyes of danger . . . we relied on each other for rightness of action, in emergencies, often without audible language between us."[7]

Don died in 1950 from pneumonia complicated by bronchial asthma, an after-effect of gassing in WWI trenches.[8] After his death, Phyllis continued to be active in the Alpine Club of Canada but did not attempt any serious climbing. Her diaries record, "I've lost my anchor . . . We are a team, and now, I have to carry on without him. I'm fifty-five years old, and I'm not sure that I can do it alone."[9]

We carried on together through the sidehilling ankle torture until the land levelled off in a grove of red alder trees. We bypassed a small, murky pond and trudged through dense underbrush before stopping to rest in a small clearing. It wasn't an ideal location for setting up camp because it lacked fresh water, but we had been hiking for five hours and found no other suitable site.

I dropped my pack to the ground, exhausted, and lay on top of the flat wooden frame. It felt good to stretch my back and look up at the clear blue sky. Every muscle of my body relaxed and I remained motionless for a good long while before sitting up on top of my pack. Some of the guys had chosen spots on the ground, but I found it was hard enough to keep clean on the trail without voluntarily sitting in the dirt.

"I need to get more water," Bryan said, pulling the cork stopper out of his canteen and shaking the empty container.

"Yeah, I need some too," said Greg. "I'm going back to that pond to get water to filter." He rummaged through his pack to pull out a plastic bladder and went to collect the water.

"For lunch we have sardines," Bryan announced to the rest of us. He tossed a can to Joe and one to Stuart, and I took one from him.

A few minutes later Greg came back with the bladder full of cloudy brown water. He hung it from a tree and attached the filter tubing to another bladder to receive the purified water with the help of gravity.

"Sardines?" Bryan offered him.

"Oh, is there anything else? I don't like sardines," Greg replied. Joe rolled his eyes.

"Sure, what about tuna?" said Bryan, much obliging.

"Thanks." Greg accepted the can.

The team takes a break in the forest after a long, hard morning of hiking. Photo by Greg Gransden.

We ate our meal straight out of the cans. Greg offered to fill our canteens with clean water from his filter and we accepted, having no other option. Up to now, we hadn't had much trouble finding fresh water from creeks trickling down from the high mountain glaciers. Other than boiling water for cooking, we'd been drinking water directly from these clear streams without any kind of filter. The risk of contamination was low, but it was a risk nonetheless.

The team's rudimentary food storage system consists of emptying cans from the packs onto piles on the forest floor.

After a good hour's rest, we emptied our loads in a pile on the ground and started back for Jewakwa Camp, Stuart taking the lead as navigator. He was skillful in retracing our routes through the woods, though always with a slight degree of variation. Joe travelled on a parallel path along the ridge to assist with navigation, calling out every so often to report on what he saw. The air was heavy with humidity, and the sweltering heat in the flats of the forest was almost unbearable. The underbrush was thick with ferns and vine maple bushes, obscuring the view ahead. I stayed close to Bryan, Greg, and Stuart. Without a trail or any landmarks and dense forest in every direction, it was easy to become disorientated.

"I found the water!" I heard Joe yell out a while later. We shifted direction to join him at the rock outcrop and fill our canteens. I paused to take in the still quiet of the forest, punctuated only by the musical notes of the water bouncing off the silvery grey granitic rock.

Once again, Joe veered off on a parallel route to Stuart. I couldn't see him but heard his occasional cursing at branches.

"Joe?" Bryan called, trying to keep tabs on everyone in the group.

"Yep, I'm about thirty feet below you," Joe replied.

Another half hour passed. Bryan, Greg, and I were behind Stuart, following a faint dirt trail no bigger than a footpath through the low-lying greenery. We hadn't heard from Joe in a while, so Bryan called out, "Hey, Joe!"

Joe replied something indistinguishable on the slope below. We all stopped to listen more closely. I could barely make out his voice through the trees. Bryan called out again, "Joe, where are you?"

I strained my ears. After a long pause came the words, "I fell."

My mind jumped to conclusions. Had he tumbled down the slope? Was he hurt? I threw Bryan a worried look.

"Come up to us," Bryan called.

We waited in silence, perched on the wisp of a trail on the side of the hill. Joe did not come.

"Joe, where are you?" Bryan shouted, a muscle in his jaw twitching with impatience.

"I'm fine," grumbled Joe's voice through the trees. "I'll meet you at camp."

Joe's refusal to join us was irrational. We were still a good hour from camp. Bryan's face was turning a deep, angry red. "We are staying together," he bellowed.

We waited anxiously for ten minutes for Joe to make his way up the hill. He finally appeared, looking somewhat bedraggled, and drifted forward to slump against a tree. Bryan was fuming. "What the hell are you thinking? We need to stay together," he scolded. "Now let's go."

But Joe didn't budge, only muttered something incomprehensible. I heard a "no" somewhere in there. He caught his breath. "Need a few minutes."

We waited. Joe was acting surly and uncooperative. Throwing up his arms in exasperation, Bryan gave up on reasoning with him. He started stalking his way back to Jewakwa Camp. The rest of us trailed behind him, leaving Joe sitting on a rock on the thin path in the forest.

It was early evening when we arrived at camp. We expected Joe to have beat us back since he hiked faster alone than in the group and sometimes took shortcuts. But Joe was not there. I figured he was probably right behind us. In the meantime we busied ourselves with our camp tasks.

An hour later Joe still had not returned, and soon it would be dark. I began to worry. There was no way for us to communicate with him if he was lost. Searching for him would be futile since he could have taken any number of routes and we had no flashlights to see in the dark. Bryan paced around the fire, his expression switching between livid and genuinely concerned. The List of Doom had warned us about making poor decisions under the stress of fatigue or thirst. Leaving Joe behind had been one of those, and Bryan was probably kicking himself for it. Stuart, Greg, and I also shouldered part of the blame. We all knew better. Now all we could do was wait.

Just before dark, Joe finally came sauntering up the trail, looking relaxed and in better spirits. He smiled when he saw Stuart, and I hurried to greet him.

"Hey, Joe. Oh man, we were getting worried," Stuart said.

"Are you okay? What happened?" I asked.

The three of us stood in the middle of camp as Joe recounted his misadventure. He'd gotten lost and run out of water, and heat exhaustion had set in. That explained his baffling, combative behaviour.

"So I headed downhill," he told us. "I figured if I could make it to the river, I could get some water. I drank and cooled off and felt much better. I even got to explore and climb a little. Then I followed the river back to camp."

I was flooded with relief that Joe had made it safely back. Without any navigational tools other than the sun and his general sense of orientation, Joe had enough outdoor experience to know that since water flows downhill, that was his key to finding the Jewakwa River. And by following the river he would eventually reach the Jewakwa bridge, a clear landmark to the location of our camp. He had escaped his ordeal by being self-reliant and using his wilderness survival skills. Even so, his close call with disaster could have been avoided had our group been better at communicating and looking out for each other.

Joe always finds his way through the forest. Photo by Greg Gransden.

Bryan didn't speak with Joe but kept to his station by the campfire, sullen. Though the incident had ended fairly well, it added to the list of frustrations that seemed to be growing between the two men. We all took our plates, piled on the beans and sausage Bryan had made, and sat around the fire to eat. Joe and Stuart chatted about Joe's experience teaching high school kids, about Stuart's daughters and life at home in the small town of Arnprior, Ontario. I listened incredulously to the banal banter—there was nothing about how either had felt about the day's perturbing events.

I had envisioned that this expedition would bond us through a common ordeal, that we would support each other emotionally and check in on how we were handling the demands of the trail. This had been my experience on previous climbing trips with other women, who encouraged each other when the going got tough. On this trek, I was having to content myself with heart-to-hearts with my journal. We were all mired in our own private frustrations; nobody was talking about what really mattered.

Mutual trust was critical in the wilderness, especially when we found ourselves in difficult situations. By now, we had gained confidence in our team's physical ability to deal with the rigours of the trail; however, we hadn't coalesced enough to handle personality conflicts. It was evident from the first few days of the expedition: when the gear was falling apart and the team was dropping members, the men reacted with frustration, anger, and arguments. We needed leadership to mediate conversations and make sure that each member felt valued and heard. Joe was making an effort to bring up his worries, albeit in a critical way. His continued outbursts were a symptom of feeling overlooked. Greater compassion and co-operation were indispensable if we were going to overcome the team's discord.

I took a sip of my tea. The heat of the cup in my hand radiated through me like a warm hug. Joe and Stuart's laughter brought my attention back to the campfire and I smiled along with them. Then I realized, we *were* in the act of building social bonds, gathered around the fire, drinking tea and coffee, having a smoke. We were just connecting differently from how women like me connected. I was surrounded by men. It made sense that we were not going to be talking about our feelings.

I suddenly understood how our actions, too, demonstrated emotional support, and a flush of appreciation washed over me. Putting a pot of coffee on the fire wasn't just preparing a drink but an invitation to relax together in the safety of camp. Dressing a wound wasn't just a medical task but protecting others from further injury. Singing songs on the trail wasn't simply to scare the bears away but a way to share a happy feeling. Airing out a tentmate's sleeping bag wasn't just keeping a tidy camp but a reciprocal gesture of gratitude. I hadn't noticed that these ordinary acts, words aside, forged the bonds of trust in our group. Because the valley was so taxing, we could only exist in this place together. Forgetting that, everything breaks down, conflict arises, and we cannot move. The path becomes impenetrable even if it isn't the forest that is standing in our way.

Chapter Eight

A Day Off

THE SPRINGY ALDER TREES' SUPPLE BRANCHES bent easily at my touch. I was careful not to let them whip Bryan in the face, who was walking behind me through the woods. Pushing aside a last branch, I squinted in the sudden bright sunlight flooding the astonishing scene before me. The milky Homathko River rushed by under massive mountains and the distant snowfields of Whitemantle Glacier. The faint footpath we'd been following hadn't given us any clues that the river was so near. A cool breeze wafted off the glacial waters, refreshing me.

"Look at that view," Bryan exclaimed. "Let's take a minute here to rest."

We let down our packs on the sandy clearing, and Greg pulled out his camera to film the surroundings. Like a bench in an art gallery, a beached log invited us to contemplate the landscape. Bryan and I took a seat.

The Homathko River in the lap of Whitemantle Glacier, as witnessed by the author's 1921 Kodak camera.

"You see there?" Bryan pointed his ice axe up toward the serrated mountain ridge. "On the other side of that ridge is Waddington Glacier." Our climbing support team would soon be meeting us at its toe.

I imagined what the glacier might look like, what immeasurable distance stretched between us. All the features of this valley seemed enormous.

Joe had wandered over to the opposite side of the clearing to investigate something that had caught his eye. Partially hidden by trees, he found a derelict yellow logging truck.

"Bryan, how much further do you think we have?" Greg asked, putting down his camera.

"If all goes according to plan, Mark and Ron R. should be flying in today," Bryan said. "We probably have fifteen or twenty kilometres left to reach them."

"We've been going non-stop for two weeks," Stuart said, stating the obvious.

"I know. And that's why I think we should take a rest day tomorrow. We can recoup our energies before making our last push to the glacier."

"It'll be nice to do some laundry," I remarked, pulling at my shirt and wrinkling my nose. It hadn't been washed in ten days. With only one set of hiking clothes, laundering required a day off at camp for drying time.

"What are Mark and Ron going to do?" asked Greg. "We won't be there for days."

Bryan nodded, his slumped shoulders betraying a note of defeat. "There's not much we can do. At the pace we've been moving I figure another four days. We should still have a good week before our helicopter pickup on the 30th. Once we hit the logging road again near the Homathko bridge, we should be able to make better progress." He gave Greg a wan smile. "Can you send Ron a message? *We won't reach Scar Mountain until July 23.*" With knitted brows, Greg pulled out his SPOT device and typed the message on the tiny phone-sized keyboard.

Bryan stood up, signalling the break was over. "I think we should try to find a campsite further along, keep an eye out for a water source," he said. The creeks that flowed down the mountainsides were clearer and safer to drink than the silty Homathko.

We picked up our packs and continued down the fuzzy-edged footpath, plunging back into the forest to follow a shallow channel of the river. During the spring melt season the channel would be running much higher, but in midsummer it lay low in the riverbed, flowing so calmly it hardly looked like it was moving. The sloping mountain on our right, barely visible under its mantle of shrubbery, offered us a narrow ten-foot landing before the river's edge. It was easy enough to spot a creek trickling down the slope to form a small pool at its base. Bryan decided we should camp among the woodland ferns populating the riverbank. I called our spot Fernbed by the River.

As evening fell over the valley, we lingered in a circle around the fire. Sitting comfortably on the soft earth, Bryan stirred pasta in one pot and emptied cans of tomato sauce and corned beef into the cast iron skillet. A new favourite dish had emerged: corned beef spaghetti. After a day of hiking and sweating, our bodies lapped up the saltiness of the canned meat.

"I'm glad you're enjoying the spaghetti bolognese à la corned beef," Bryan said with a coy smile. We nodded without looking up from our bowls. "If we had met up with Mark and Ron today as scheduled, you would have been eating steaks right now."

"No way!" Joe exclaimed.

Bryan chuckled. "Yeah, I wanted to surprise you with fresh steaks, so I had Mark and Ron chopper them in for us."

"That's just our luck," I said good-naturedly. Nothing seemed to surprise me anymore.

The idea of a celebratory meal lifted our spirits even if we weren't able to enjoy it. After dinner, Bryan opened his Tiffany blue tin of tobacco for his pipe.

"Hey, Bryan," Joe said, "do you think I can use some of your tobacco? I'm out of my stash."

"Sure, help yourself," Bryan replied in his usual genial manner.

If Joe was going to make a habit of borrowing from Bryan's limited supply of tobacco, I hoped this wasn't going to create further grievances between them.

The following day was ours to do with as we pleased. I was looking forward to cleaning and recuperating. The first thing I did after a breakfast of easy oatmeal and coffee was tidy up inside the tent I shared with Bryan. I draped our two sleeping bags over a long branch to air them out, even though there wasn't any breeze nor much sun filtering down through the dense canopy of the trees. Nearby, Bryan was turning over a large pot on the ground.

"What are you going to do today?" I asked him.

"I'm planning to bake biscuits," he said, his eyes sparkling with anticipation. We had plenty of flour but little time to prepare quick breads and bannock as he'd intended.

I fetched the wash basin and my toiletries and walked fifty feet downriver to designate a plump bush as a bathing spot. First was to dip the basin into the river and pull up a heavy pailful of silty water. After waiting for the sediment to settle, I bent over the basin to lather my hair and body with my all-in-one bar of soap. Washing from a bucket was better than my usual daily wipe-down but not as good as the clear pool we'd bathed in at Mosquito Camp. I dried off with my hand towel and pulled on my union suit. Then it was my clothes' turn to be washed. Greg hopped on the laundry train too. Since Bryan was busy with his cooking project, I asked him if he wanted anything washed.

"You don't need to do my laundry," he said sheepishly.

I waved my hand to dismiss his comment and waited expectantly.

"Okay, my shirt and a pair of socks. I'll get them for you."

The Munday party also had a wash day when they were midway through the valley. Phyllis and Thomas took on the task of doing the team's laundering. They were incredulous to discover that Johnnie, a bachelor, had brought no less than sixteen pairs of socks and multiple suits of underwear he planned to throw away rather than wash.[1]

Meanwhile, Bryan was kneeling at the pile of food to gather his ingredients: flour, baking powder, butter. Stuart and Joe were about to head off to scout ahead on the trail.

"Hey, Stuart, do you know where the butter is?" Bryan asked, eyeballing the provisions. "I don't see the tin."

"Beats me," Stuart answered. "I just know that I stashed the lard at Mountainview Camp."

Bryan turned to frown at Stuart. "No, no, *I* stashed the lard. We agreed we didn't need both. I saw a tin left behind and thought you had forgotten to stash it in the hole in the rock wall."

"Nope, it was one of the first things I stashed," Stuart replied.

They looked at each other for a moment, then realization dawned on their faces. I chuckled quietly.

"So now I have no butter or lard." Bryan scratched his head and resigned himself to the blunder. He scanned the stockpile for an alternative and landed on the tin of peanut butter. "This will have to do," he said.

To make biscuits, Bryan needed to fashion a device to bake them in. An enamel plate set like a cookie sheet inside a deep-walled pot was the beginnings of an oven. Now he needed something to use as a lid to distribute the heat. Greg and I were heading to the clearing along the Homathko River to dry our clothing in the breeze, and Bryan tagged along to see if he could find a useful item around the abandoned logging truck.

Fifteen minutes down the trail, we emerged from under the canopy of the forest to be greeted by the brilliant sun. I draped the wet garments on tree stumps and hung the socks in the branches of a small bush while Bryan poked around the truck.

A derelict old logging truck sitting on its own in the wilderness near Fernbed by the River Camp.

Greg and I meandered over to the art gallery log to relax under the mountainous landscape. I breathed in the fresh air and my tensions melted away. Finally clean after my bath, I was feeling more like myself again. This clearing was another oasis amid the stifling woods. I watched the Homathko River rush past, voluminous even in midsummer. The snowfields over the distant mountains seemed to belong to another world. I knew it would be cold and icy once we got there, and I wasn't sure I had enough warm clothes. But I dismissed the thought. At the snail's pace we were moving, how far would we get?

"Do you think we're going to make it to the glacier?" I asked Greg.

"I don't know. This whole trip has been crazy. So many things have gone wrong," he said. "There's supposed to be another section of the old logging road somewhere close."

I closed my eyes as I lay on the log. "Hmm. I hope we find it soon."

"If we don't we'll end up wandering around like last time."

I nodded and stared off at the mountain. As much as it would have been nice to have a conversation, I was enjoying the quiet time to reflect. During the long hours of hiking, it took all my energy to step carefully on the uneven terrain, mount over logs, thwack through branches. I was constantly monitoring my hydration and energy levels and paying attention to keep up with the group. Basking in the sunshine on the log, I finally had some time to mull things over and try to understand why there were so many tensions between the team members.

I wondered if Bryan and the rest of us had planned thoroughly enough to have a reasonable shot at climbing the mountain. In the months of preparations leading up to the expedition, Bryan's responses to questions from the team members were at times flippant. When asked what the Mundays did to protect themselves from rain, he answered, "They just got wet." We were fortunate that Stuart and Joe had brought tools for repair work and tarps for the tent floors. I understood that antiquated equipment would make our experience more challenging; however, I didn't think we should be purposefully skimping on preparations and putting ourselves at a disadvantage simply to experience how tough and resilient the Mundays were. The valley was challenging enough without any added hindrances. There was a disconnect I couldn't quite figure out.

Every day as I hiked through the valley I asked myself, *what are we doing here?* Our expedition's success was purportedly rooted in a singular goal, which was to climb Mount Waddington using period gear. This was the lofty aim Bryan had promoted to our sponsors and supporters. But we were also following in the footsteps of the Mundays, who valued exploring the whole of the mountain environment, not just its crests. Don rejected mountaineers' narrow emphasis on claiming peaks. "I am very happy on a glacier," he wrote, "and do not intend to be robbed of that joy by [modern people] who think mostly in terms of peaks. . . . [Mountain] passes once were goals a climber might seek without loss of prestige."[2] If we passed near the mountain without reaching its summit, would this make our efforts any less respectable or somehow a failure?

We'd come into the valley with two conflicting goals, which I thought might explain the friction between Joe and Bryan. Our main purpose was either to climb Mystery

Mountain or to do as the Mundays had done and discover what the path toward the mountain had to offer.

If our priority was to climb the mountain, once we'd realized that the bushwhacking would take longer than the ten days we'd allocated, we could have chartered a helicopter to whisk us up to the glacier, just like the Arc'teryx team had chosen to do in their 2016 expedition. They could also have opted to stay true to the Mundays' limitations and continue on foot, even though they were low on food and risked not making it to Mount Waddington.

I recalled what Bryan had told me when he first explained his motivations for the expedition: *We've lost the pioneering explorers' spirit of adventure, their resilience and self-sufficiency.* From this perspective, the point of the expedition was to gain an appreciation of the challenges faced by Canada's early explorers. If the Munday spirit was what we were principally after, it wouldn't make sense to give up on the hike through the valley for the glory of the mountain summit; climbing Mount Waddington could only be a secondary goal. Pathfinding in dense coastal bush, ferrying heavy pack loads, run-ins with bears, incessant mosquitoes: these were the same challenges the Mundays faced in 1926. Our hike in the valley could not be rushed or cheated through or done haphazardly because those very obstacles made up the Munday experience.

I emerged from my reverie to check that the clothes had dried, and Greg and I walked back to Fernbed by the River Camp. Stuart and Joe had returned from their scouting. Bryan guarded a plateful of fluffy, fresh-baked biscuits, seeing the rest of us circling around.

"No, not yet. You'll have to wait for dinner," he said.

He had found a circular piece of scrap metal to fit onto his makeshift oven as a lid. It had curved edges, making it an ideal receptacle for hot coals. Building the oven, mixing up the dough, and baking a dozen biscuits had taken him the better part of the day.

I took the sleeping bags into my tent to rest some more. The blisters on my shoulder were still painfully red and angry-looking. Mixing a bit of salt into a bowl of cool water and dipping my cotton bandana into it, I made myself a saltwater compress and tended to my injuries until dinner. The quiet day had cleared my thoughts and rejuvenated my body.

It was with high anticipation of fresh-baked treats that we congregated around the campfire that evening. We hadn't had any bread for over a week. But Bryan prefaced the meal by saying, "I think we should ration the biscuits over the next few days." Our eager expressions deflated. Bryan was either spent from baking all day or our dinner choices were dwindling. Dinner consisted of canned beans with some sausage thrown in; on the side, we each were given one half of a biscuit. He was serious about rationing those biscuits. We nevertheless devoured our shares. Curiously, they didn't taste like peanut butter at all.

Our post-dinner wind-down involved cigarette rolling for Joe, pipe smoking for Bryan, and coffee for Stuart and me. Greg didn't drink coffee and opted for tea instead. Joe and Stuart filled us in on their exploits of the day: the trail rose a few hundred feet up a hillside to an overlook peeking down on the Homathko River, a perfect spot to camp. Joe relished in the freedom of scouting as a respite from the daily drudgery of hauling heavy packs back and forth. The dense green canopy of the woods was starting to get monotonous.

"This is killing me," he confided to us, sitting cross-legged on the forest floor. "I want to explore, climb, and touch the mountain. I'm tired of carrying loads through the bush. We should be hiking longer, getting further if we really want to make it." He set down his coffee cup and gazed at the ground. "I'm . . . not sure everyone really trained for this."

Bryan and Stuart stared at him blankly. Indignation welled up in me as if I'd been directly targeted. I heard the words flow out of my mouth, calm and confident.

"I trained for this every single day." I pointed to Bryan—"Bryan trained"—then Stuart—"Stuart trained. That's just not true."

A silence fell over us. For the better part of this trip I'd been quiet and accommodating, keeping up and pulling my weight and doing everything expected of me as a dutiful team member. But I was feeling more capable as a woodswoman now, and after the day's reflections, my mind was clear. I had regained my capacity to react and make myself heard. I understood that we were all trying to make sense of our situation however we could. Joe seemed to lash out and cast blame when he was feeling powerless. I felt it too.

We spent the next day delivering the bulk of our provisions and climbing equipment to the overlook, covering the food with the usual tarp before heading back to Fernbed by the River Camp for another night. We returned to the overlook around midday on July 21 with the last of our gear. From the heights of our vantage point we could see the Homathko River wind its way into the distance and disappear around Scar Mountain.

Instead of the deep blue sky I had expected, a heavy haze hung over the mountains, even though the day wasn't humid or particularly hot. The air felt refreshingly cool at this elevation, and the mosquitoes were nowhere to be seen. I dubbed the overlook Balcony Camp.

Bryan watches the cooking pot at Balcony Camp, which overlooks the Homathko River.

Our team set to work, now efficient at the tasks of chopping wood, fashioning poles and setting up tents, digging a latrine, and fetching water. Bryan rummaged through the food stores for the biscuits to make sandwiches. Discovering an empty sack littered with crumbs, he exclaimed, "Oh man. They're all gone." The delicious products of a day's labour had been stolen by critters.

Disappointed, we plunked ourselves down in a circle on the wiry grass to make do with what we had. Bryan held a tin of corned beef upside down to slide the meat out onto a plate and cut it into wedges. We had our sandwiches nonetheless, using slices of cheese as the bread.

Up until this point, we hadn't encountered any wildlife raiding our food at camp. Perhaps we'd been a bit complacent in leaving those tasty morsels unattended at a cache. The aroma must have been irresistible to the forest creatures, who had a grand time feasting on our prized biscuits.

Chapter Nine

Torment and Surrender

WE LEFT BALCONY CAMP on July 22, descending the ridge to follow the Homathko River through compact groves of young alders, thin and springy, which flourished in the lowlands along the water. Even the faint footpath we'd been tracing had disappeared. The shoreline pushed up against the trees for the most part, but sometimes widened into sandy flats created by the accumulation of glacial sediment carried down by the river in the spring. Where the alders were too tightly clustered, Stuart led the way out of the bush to walk these short sandbars, providing a welcome change of scenery. Our hobnail boots made temporary imprints on the wet sand alongside deeply embedded cougar tracks.

Stepping out onto one of these patches of waterlogged sand, Stuart witnessed his boot slowly beginning to sink. In keeping with his character, he didn't get too excited, but Joe, like the town crier, announced, "Hey, we found quicksand here!"

It was impossible to tell where the quicksand lay just by looking at it. Prodding it curiously with the toe of my boot, I found it had a peculiar viscosity, bouncy at first, then slowly giving way to suck at my boot. Here was another item I mentally checked off the List of Doom.

Following the path of least resistance, we soon found ourselves on higher ground, entering a more mature mixed forest of alders and hemlocks. We crunched over a thick brown carpet of dry leaves and twigs through the trees, the uneven terrain wreaking havoc on my sore ankles. Suddenly, I heard yelps of pain and saw Stuart running erratically with arms flailing as if trying to escape. A short while later Bryan jumped about in a frenzy, and then it was Joe and Greg who burst into fits of crazed, spastic running. I gave a wide berth to the scene. A secret danger lay under the cloak of debris on the forest floor. Stuart had stepped near a hornets' nest, and one by one, the guys had been assailed. This forest was like a minefield. Later at camp we would laugh at Stuart's misfortune of having been stung on his right nipple.

The day stretched on, Stuart and Joe taking us in and out of hornet-infested woods and through dense thickets of young alders flourishing with greenery. Under the springy stalks of the ten-foot trees, I felt like an ant meandering through an endless grassy lawn. Joe's simple navigation system was to keep the river to our left and the mountain to our right. Other than catching brief glimpses of the water from high points on a ridgeline, we were groping our way blindly through the woods. My field of view was limited to a few feet before me, much like walking in the dark with a flashlight. I concentrated on keeping close to the group. Some sections of brush crowded so closely together that we had to skirt around them. And sometimes it was easier to climb over tangles of fallen trees like jungle gyms, possibly left over from a clear-cut decades ago.

Bryan hikes across giant fallen logs in the forest. Photo by Greg Gransden.

Four hours later, we were surprised to emerge from the bush to once again meet the Homathko River under sunny skies. Following its course, we decided to set up camp at a clearing where an old, dried-up river seemed to have once flowed into the Homathko. An intricate pile of bleached grey logs stood in the shallow water near the shore. We could have mistaken the arrangement for a natural phenomenon had the logs not been stacked high in a distinctively organized way. Like children we climbed over the floating playground, and I snapped photos of the place I named Driftwood Camp.

After the tents were set up, the guys had a communal bathing session in the shallows. They stood together naked, talking and splashing water on themselves. Feeling self-conscious, I walked downriver behind the heap of driftwood to wash my shirt and clean up. Once the splashing sounds had died down I scrambled onto the logs to lay out my shirt to dry in the sun, then dangled my feet in the cool water to soothe my swollen ankles.

The author soothes her swollen ankles in the cool water, sitting atop a pile of driftwood on the shore of the Homathko River. Photo by Greg Gransden.

While Bryan was preparing dinner, he asked Greg to message Mark and Ron R. again. Instead of meeting them tomorrow as we'd previously estimated, we anticipated a delay of three more days. Meanwhile, Joe went to scout ahead in preparation for the next day's hike. He returned as if he had just gone on an evening stroll, looking relaxed and content. Scouting definitely agreed with him. He reported what he'd seen: "We're okay for a while, then we hit this massive jungle gym up a hillside. It's like a maze of death."

As I heard Joe say *maze of death*, I was stricken with apprehension. I had proved to myself that I could carry my heavy pack on low-lying hills, but could I do it up sheer mountainsides? We hadn't yet encountered much elevation gain. Images of deepest, thickest forests on punishingly steep slopes sprang to my mind. It would be a terrible struggle.

With the help of my journal, I greeted this old, familiar feeling of fear, which I now understood was tied to uncertainty about what lay ahead. Every day we faced uncertainty in this valley. Perseverance through fear, I'd learned, was a choice I could make. Dread and self-doubt still visited me but rather than let them stop me in my tracks, I focused on what I was able to do in the present moment. As the day waned, photographing the surrounding mountains and taking part in camp life kept my mind attuned to the here and now.

The next day, July 23, I readied myself for the maze of death, wrapping my ankles with tension bandages for added support and eating a hearty breakfast of oatmeal. With my nerves slightly on edge, I loaded my pack, picked up my long-handled ice axe for a walking stick, and followed Stuart and Joe through the wilderness. The forest was thick and claustrophobic but passable. Dead branches thrusting out of the tree trunks stabbed at our arms and legs. One of these ripped a hole in my shirt at the chest pocket. And then, after an hour of hiking, the forest canopy came to an abrupt end. We'd reached the maze of death.

Spreading across the forty-five degree slope of Landmark Mountain was a labyrinthine mass of deadfall as far as the eye could see. There seemed to be no wind, no sound at all. It was as if a swath of forest had been swiped from the mountainside, chewed up, and spit out with a bunch of boulders thrown in for good measure. Above our heads the sky was a muted blue, and the sun shone weakly over an enormous graveyard of bleached old logs teetering on top of each other, their scraggly branches dry and brittle. Avalanche debris hadn't been mentioned on the List of Doom, but as we were about to climb over it, I thought it should have been. New shrubs and trees had sprung forth from the spaces between the decaying logs and boulders, obscuring the sizeable gaps between the debris and the ground below.

Joe went first, then Stuart, me, and Bryan. Greg held back to get a better angle for filming. We zigzagged from log to log, climbing higher and higher up the mountainside. The ground lay in dark pits metres below the logs, and I was glad to have my ice axe to balance me out with a third point of contact.

The team starts to climb the field of avalanche debris that Joe has named the Maze of Death. Photo by Greg Gransden.

It took a good hour of carefully measured strides across the logs to approach the end of the maze. As I was stepping down from the last log my boot slipped through a hole and I was falling, my pack swinging me sideways. Instinctively, I grabbed onto a small standing tree with the sole thought, *please don't twist my ankle*. Holding on with all my strength I stopped the fall, pulled my boot out of the hole, and sighed with relief as I put it down to safety. I had escaped the maze of death.

Slanting back down the hillside, we continued deep into the woods, seeming to travel back in time to a prehistoric forest. We passed giant firs and wide-trunked red cedars that must have been growing for five hundred years, and brushed past the large fronds of woodland ferns that found their home in the moist soil of the lowlands. I was brought back to my childhood fantasies of adventure fuelled by stories such as *Journey to the Centre of the Earth*. The sun filtered down through the trees to encourage the growth of otherworldly plants standing over six feet tall on rigid stalks with mighty, maple-like leaves as wide as two feet. The inch-thick canes covered in sharp spines looked nasty. Even the undersides of the broad leaves were dressed with small spiny needles. I thought to myself, this must be the primordial devil's club that Bryan said we were sure to encounter. A distant cousin of the ginseng plant, the inner bark has been traditionally used by Indigenous peoples for its antibacterial properties. I was awestruck by the imposing plant but warily followed the List of Doom's advice to put on my leather gloves. Greg had seemingly not gotten the memo to bring gloves and got a handful of these spines. Later, back at Driftwood Camp, Stuart got out his tweezers and tended to Greg's hand, pulling out the noxious and irritating needles.

Day by day we inched our way toward Mystery Mountain, ferrying loads over increasingly rougher terrain. The maze of death, we discovered, was only the beginning. The overgrown logging road seemed like a walk in the park compared to the following day's hike on July 24. We faced a mountainside that plunged directly into the Homathko, so we had no choice but to sidehill our way across, high above the river. The forty-five degree slope was littered with enormous fallen cedars, and we climbed over or crawled under hundred-foot trunks that seemed to block our way every twenty feet. My technique was to embed the pick end of my ice axe in the log as an anchor, gain my footing on the bark, and swing my leg over like I was mounting a horse. Glancing down a hundred feet below, I saw the river flowing by, unconcerned. The valley was revealing itself for what it truly was: wild, rough, and unforgiving.

Bryan uses his ice axe as a hold to climb over a massive tree on a steep mountain slope. Photo by Greg Gransden.

Eventually, the mountain slope levelled off and we came to the edge of a limpid freshwater stream with a bed of round river rocks tucked underneath the surface. A log bridge lay at an upward angle across the fifteen-foot stream to reach the higher bank on the other side. After nearly three weeks of hiking over tree trunks, I was feeling more confident in log crossings. We found ourselves on a small island backed by a broad waterfall set into the mountainside. Twin streams flowed from the base of the falls and almost completely surrounded the small island before joining the Homathko River. The tall cedars that inhabited the island were widely spaced, ideal for pitching tents. Glacier-cooled air coming off the river discouraged most of the mosquitoes; a large bench-like log in the centre was the perfect spot for Bryan to set up the firepit. I called this spectacular location Cedar Camp.

After a dinner of battered bacon, we enjoyed the evening. Perched on the log bench, Bryan studied his map, trying to determine where our camp was located. He and Stuart were fairly confident we were within ten kilometres of Mark and Ron R. on the other side of Scar Mountain, at the toe of Waddington Glacier. We just had to make it past a spur of Landmark Mountain. On the other side of the big bend, the Homathko bridge would be easy enough to find as we picked up the logging road again. Feeling the time crunch before our July 30 helicopter pickup, Bryan was determined to reach the Homathko bridge the next day.

We woke early on July 25, packed a load, and left our little island over another log bridge on the other side. In the kilometre-wide expanse between the Homathko River and the slopes of Landmark Mountain, we wound our way around tall firs and cedars and bushwhacked through leafy thickets that threatened to entangle us. Stuart was once again at the head of the group, choosing our way forward. He had inadvertently led the expedition for much of the way, come to the rescue when things needed fixing, and carried the heaviest loads without ever a word of complaint. Close behind him, Joe veered off in another direction and Bryan hesitated. Pointing between the two directions, he called to Stuart, "Which way are we going?"

Stuart glanced sideways and brusquely said, "Follow me or not, I don't care."

I was taken aback by his uncharacteristic reaction. Stuart was always so even-tempered and calm. I suppose the stress of leading through the bush half blind was beginning to wear on him.

As the hours trickled by and we edged closer to the spur, the wide woods between the mountain and the river narrowed. The early afternoon sun squinted through the trees to dapple moss-covered boulders and ferns sprouting wherever they could take root. Mosses hung off the tree branches, giving them the appearance of weeping. The steeply rising mountain slope was funnelling us into a thin strip of riverbank no more than four feet wide. Finally, we arrived at a colossal heap of fallen old-growth trees that blocked our way. It looked as if giants had been playing with matchsticks. We stopped before this impasse and dropped our packs.

Bryan surveys the enormous blockage of fallen old-growth trees that pins us in between the mountainside and the river.

Bryan tried to heave himself up the massive logs, pushing aside hanging mosses, but they were too high to climb over. He returned to us, his face grave. We were pinned in.

"Stuart, maybe you can scramble up the hillside to see a way around this blockage," he suggested.

"Sure, I won't be long," Stuart replied.

Joe slumped down against his pack and stared blankly into his lap as he twisted a twig around. At the river's edge, Bryan sat against a tree, his eyes fixed on the blockage. If we couldn't get past this roadblock and reach the Homathko bridge, we would be delayed again and possibly never reach the alpine.

Greg got his camera out and filmed our dejected faces. We hadn't had lunch, so I pulled out some nuts from my haversack and shared them with the others. Taking my cue, Bryan sliced pieces of summer sausage, and we solemnly ate by the river.

Joe and Bryan wearily listen to Stuart report what lies beyond the barrier of trees. Photo by Greg Gransden.

After an hour, Stuart came sidling down the rocky slope, shirtless and sweaty. "This mess extends at least another kilometre or more," he reported. "The only way to avoid it is to go up a thousand feet and back down."

We were already disheartened by our slow progress, and now Stuart's bad news confirmed that we had lost the day. It was as if the forest was telling us, *that's far enough*. The fallen trees were like fingers of an enormous hand stopping us from going forward. There was no space to make camp on the narrow riverbank, and it was getting too late to ferry more loads to this point. We decided to leave a cache of our belongings in the rocks and return back to our camp at Cedar Island.

I woke the next morning, July 26, full of renewed energy after a good night's sleep and ready to tackle the day. If the only way to get past the blockage was to climb up, then I was ready to climb. As Bryan prepared breakfast, I was the first to take down the tent, roll up our sleeping bags, and be ready to go. We were within reach of the alpine, and we could make it within our four remaining days before our helicopter pickup.

Joe felt otherwise. He moved slowly through camp, poured himself some coffee, and sprawled on the ground, leaning against a cedar. "I'm not going anywhere today," he said. "I need a rest."

"We have four days left. We can still make it," said Bryan from his spot on the ground, trying to be encouraging.

The night before, Greg had notified Mark and Ron R. that we were still ten kilometres away. Having failed to reach the Homathko bridge, our arrival was delayed yet again, and it was becoming clear that we were not going to climb any mountains further up the glacier. This had been the last straw for Joe.

"There's no point in continuing on," Joe said to Bryan in a low, monotone voice. "I don't see the point. We're going to push so hard to get ourselves out of the valley, for the sake of getting out of the valley? I came here to climb a mountain. That's gone now."

Bryan blinked rapidly. "We get past the blockage today and catch the logging road over the last bridge, and the rest of the way up Scar Creek is easy. We may have a day or two to climb the glaciers."

Joe stood up to refill his coffee and moved to the log bench opposite Bryan. "We aren't going to reach our goal. So why push further?" he repeated. "We carried heavy packs through the bush. How great for us," he said sarcastically, raising his eyebrows. The pitch of his voice began to rise as he worked himself up into a frenzied monologue, unleashing his frustrations on Bryan. "I've held my tongue long enough. This is all you get from me. That's it. I have no more to give." He sipped some more coffee resolutely.

Bryan sat stooped over, his elbows on his knees and his hands clasped before him, listening to Joe.

"I told you from day three," Joe shouted, "day fucking three, that things needed to change. Now at day twenty-one, -two, -five, I don't know, we're out of time."

Joe's latest reproach was enough to take Bryan to his breaking point. He stood up and erupted into a countertirade. "How selfish can you be? Thinking that you can unilaterally decide it's all over?"

"I have given everything to this expedition. I've been getting up early, trying to light a fire under everyone's ass. And you know what, I haven't felt taken care of. My concerns haven't been heard since day one."

Bryan scowled and shook his head. "It's always about you, Joe!"

They were now standing in a face-to-face confrontation, arms gesticulating as they shouted accusations at each other. Nothing was held back. Stuart, Greg, and I watched in a ring around the spectacle like we were at a boxing match. Greg pulled out his phone to film the unfolding scene, but Joe grabbed it from his hands and threw it into the bushes. Greg ran to get his video camera to continue filming. Stuart and I tried to interject calming words, but neither Joe nor Bryan would listen. We stepped back and gave them a wider berth to let their anger run its course.

After the shouting stopped, Joe and Bryan strode off in separate directions to brood on their own. Since Bryan did not return to his campfire post, Greg, Stuart, and I scrounged around for lunch, finding leftover split pea soup. Later, Stuart busied himself by making a hammock with rope strung between two trees. I could have spent the day taking photos had I not left my camera bag at the cache by the blockage. Worried about my equipment and disappointed that we had not yet left the valley, I poured out my thoughts to my journal instead. The images I'd envisioned of alpine panoramas with specks of men climbing across the slopes were drifting out of reach. I wouldn't be capturing the mountains with my 1921 Kodak No. 2 folding camera like Phyllis had. My photography project felt like a failure.

The day after the big showdown, July 27, we intended to get around the blockage of trees and reach the Homathko bridge. Joe was not enthusiastic, still believing it was pointless, but agreed to come along. As we were having breakfast, Greg came to the campfire with his SPOT device.

"Hey guys, I just received a message from Renee," he said, looking down to read. "It says, *Helicopter needed for fire duty, can you be ready to evacuate today?*"

The news dazed Bryan momentarily, his spoonful of oatmeal frozen in mid-air. My thoughts suddenly expanded to the wider world outside our little camp in the woods. The helicopter was our lifeline, our safest way out of this wilderness. Now it was being called away. Where might the forest fire be?

Bryan clicked into gear. "We need to retrieve the cache we left yesterday," he said, thinking out loud.

"And we need to search for a spot where the helicopter can land," Stuart put in.

"Yes, we won't be able to do that all today. Okay, write them back to say we can be ready tomorrow," Bryan told Greg. "We'll send our location coordinates for pickup. Oh, and send a message to Mark and Ron telling them about our change in plans."

Greg dutifully typed out the messages on his device. Mark and Ron confirmed that they too were leaving; their helicopter pickup would be later that day. If the near-impassable bush and blockade of trees were not enough to stop us, the forest had seemingly decided to go up in flames in an effort to expel us. It was only later that I learned that 2018 was BC's third-worst wildfire season on record.[1]

We began our hike to the impasse, this time with empty packs. When we spotted a large sandbar along the Homathko River that was wide enough for a helicopter to land, Bryan decided that this would serve as our last camp and extraction site. Greg took note of the coordinates with his SPOT device.

We reached the narrow landing in front of the blockage of fallen old-growth trees. A hush fell over us as we mechanically collected our cache and filled our packs. I gave a final look to the trees, which even in death served to protect the mysteries beyond. We'd hoped to climb the formidable peaks of Mystery Mountain, but the Homathko River Valley had proved to be even tougher.

We spent the better part of the day regrouping our gear and moving camp to the place I called Pebble Beach. Its mosaic of river stones confirmed that the area had been underwater during the spring melt, when the river ran higher. The late afternoon sun cast a warm glow over the sandy flats. The riverside was airy and open and showcased the Whitemantle Range on the opposite bank. We all threw off our stinky shirts to bask in the sunshine, lounging in a circle on the sand. Joe recounted our experiences with the monster mosquitoes and the unparalleled amount of beans we'd eaten, laughing and sharing as was his specialty. Bryan stretched out on the sand, propped up by a backpack. At the fringes, Greg filmed one of the few moments in our trip that we were smiling and carefree. Once we had accepted that it was the end of the expedition, we could finally relax. To mark the moment, Stuart pulled out a special flask he'd saved for our celebratory toast on the mountain's summit.

"Tonight we have a shot of rum," he said, pouring the deep golden liquid into five cups. "I carried this rolled up in my sleeping bag the whole way."

We raised our cups together in a toast. As Joe proposed: "Here's to a mountain that's even more mysterious."

"Hear, hear," I agreed, and we each took a swig.

The team shares a celebratory toast of rum marking the end of the expedition. Photo by Greg Gransden.

It was a bittersweet end to the expedition. The warming drink complemented the warm evening air, and we sat in the sand with easy smiles.

Sleep usually came easy for me no matter how hard or lumpy the ground, but I woke in the middle of the night for no apparent reason. Opening the tent door, I was surprised to be greeted by the full moon at its zenith, beaming down on me. The timing was oddly perfect, as if the moon itself had awoken me. It cast a clear, silvery-white gaze over the land, revealing shadows and forms that by day would have been unrecognizable.

Though the massive black silhouette of the mountain ridge took up half the sky, it receded into the inky background as the quartz in the smooth, round river stones sparkled ever so subtly. By the light of the moon, the small rocks held their own magic while the grandeur of the mountains abated. The sandy flats of the Homathko River looked serene and expansive, unlike the smothered feeling I had always felt in the bush. I looked at the moon for a while and it seemed to peer back into my soul. In its reflection I recognized the fortitude I had gained, the resilience I'd shown in my quest to follow in Phyllis's footsteps. I had relied on my intuition and grounded my fears and doubts, not to ignore them but to recognize them as obstacles created by my mind. They were a part of me.

The valley, too, had placed one obstacle after another in our way. The wilderness protecting these mountains could not be so easily conquered. I understood what Don Munday meant when he wrote about Mystery Mountain, "We must return again, not as assailants, but in a spirit closer to veneration."[2] Transfixed, I watched as the glowing sphere slowly glided across the black sky and dipped below the mountain. Then I went back to sleep.

Chapter Ten

Fearless

THE HELICOPTER CAME UP THE VALLEY, a small speck at first, then as it approached, its pulsing *thump-thump-thump* got louder and louder until I could feel the sound vibrating through me. I pulled on my vintage glacier goggles to protect my eyes from the sand blowing all around me. The mechanical bird landed on the sandbank and wound itself down, and the pilot stepped out to greet us.

In the bush, moving a few kilometres took all day; actions as simple as fetching water and accessing a toilet required physical effort. This pilot was coming from the civilized world, where basic tasks of living weren't given a second thought. In this other world, vast distances were covered in minutes, water came from a tap, and waste was flushed away. I tried to remember what it was like to sleep in a bed, or lay my head on a pillow, or eat a meal sitting at a table.

Bryan crouches as the helicopter comes in for a landing to take us away from Mystery Mountain.

We piled into the helicopter and lifted off from the rocky sandbank, rising ever higher, leaving behind the earth I had been so intimate with. Aside from the physical punishment of bushwhacking with a heavy pack, this expedition also required that I accept dirt. My clothes were dirty; my sweaty body was dirty; the floorless tent was maculated with dirt; I sat in the dirt by the campfire; I even ate dirt when bits of debris floated down from the trees and landed in my food. We simply could not escape it.

High above the valley, the myopic view of the woods I'd had for the past few weeks expanded and I perceived the tapestry of the forest, the sinewy lengths of the Homathko River, and the spiked motif of snowy mountains that lay beyond our reach. Dazzled and disoriented, I scanned the carpet of trees and the curves of the mountain ridges, trying to pick out the route we had taken. It was surreal, as if the past three weeks had been only an especially lifelike dream, yet one that left real bruises and scars. My body held the memory of each kilometre we'd hiked. The sprawling valley below me receded further to blend into swaths of forest greens, milky rivers, and icy peaks. Like friends parting on a train platform, the trees and cool streams, the logs and leaves and rocks that had been with me each day disappeared into the crowd. I wondered if I would ever see them again.

The winding Homathko River, as seen from the helicopter.

A mere ten minutes later, the helicopter dropped us off at the airstrip by Homathko Camp. Before we could take up our packs, a dusty blue pickup truck rumbled up the gravel track toward us. It was Chuck, the camp manager, this time eager to greet us. He looked us over with newfound respect, visibly impressed. In a brief conversation with Bryan, he confessed that he didn't think we would last a week in the bush. Before he drove away again we told him of our plans. Greg had received confirmation that our water taxi back to Quadra Island, where we had first boarded the *Misty Isles*, was scheduled to pick us up on August 2. That left us five more days in the valley.

Bryan turned to the group, looking rather pleased with his encounter with Chuck. "All right, we have caches to collect from Mosquito and Mountainview Camp. I say we stay at Mosquito Camp since it's a nice spot and the halfway point."

Leaving our climbing gear where it lay on the grass, we packed only the essentials: tents, personal gear, some food. It took extra motivation to pick up our packs and get hiking again. One by one we headed back into the bush along the old familiar logging road.

Once again, we met the log bridge over the ravine that I had first ventured across so warily to reach Mosquito Camp. But this time, I crossed as surefooted and confident as Phyllis would have been. Past the low thickets we arrived at the sandy clearing to set up our tents. It was late morning and the sun was shining warmly. Bryan walked over to the side of the trail to check on our cache.

"Well, well, seems like the bears had a party while we were away," he said.

Our pasta, jam, and miscellaneous other foods had all been eaten. A tin of sweetened condensed milk lay empty, a hole as big as a can opener would have made where a bear claw had punctured it. We picked up the empty cans and bits of packaging and stowed them in our trash bag. The spare clothing we'd left at the cache remained intact, but the sacks in which they were stored had been pierced and torn by the bears' curious claws. I had great respect for these intelligent, though dangerously strong creatures. This was their home and I was but a visitor.

The next day, July 29, Stuart, Joe, and Greg hiked to Mountainview Camp to collect our last cache of food at the site of the butter blunder. While they were away I lazed in the shade by the pool of water, writing in my journal, soaking my sore and swollen ankles, and recuperating from the toll the bushwhacking had taken on my body, which was marked with bites, bruises, and blisters. One of these marks never faded. I later found that I'd been left with a scar on my shoulder which, curiously, is shaped like the letter *M*, a personal memento of Mystery Mountain embossed onto my skin.

For the greater part of the trip, I had struggled to live up to the legend of Phyllis Munday. What I was slowly coming to realize was how the challenges of this expedition had in fact shaped me to become more like tough, fearless Phyllis. Through my anxieties about my role in the team, the roughness of the terrain, the weight of the packs, the limitations of my sore ankles, I discovered that the two of us weren't so different after all. When she faced bears she would have felt fear, climbing for hours would have made her uncomfortable, and her arthritic knees would have given her pain. She was a woman first, suffering through the same valley, and on this level I could relate to her.

Yet as much as Phyllis too was an ordinary woman, she remained enigmatic in the breadth of her achievements. She was the only mountaineer of her era to be given honorary membership in three international mountaineering clubs, based in Britain, the US, and Canada. For her public service, she was accorded several honours and awards, the highest being the Order of Canada in 1973.[1] And I was particularly impressed with her portfolio of photographs. She accomplished much over the course of her life as a woman of her time. Phyllis died in 1990 at the age of ninety-six.

The author's 1921 Kodak camera portrays one last look at Mosquito Camp.

Unlike Phyllis, I hadn't managed to develop my own portfolio of mountain shots. Surrounded for the most part by thick walls of vegetation, it had been hard enough to see the way ahead, never mind capture sweeping vistas of glaciers. This extra time in the valley was nevertheless my last chance to travel back in time with my 1921 Kodak No. 2 folding camera. I left the bathing pool to shoot a few last photographs further up the river, close to the waterfall. For a couple of glorious hours I was lost in the colours and textures of the landscape. To see what my antique camera had recorded, I would have to wait to get home and develop the film.

I wandered back to camp to find that Bryan had made big cake-like doughnuts the size of our bowls. Having read in Don's book that doughnuts were one of Phyllis's specialties, he'd used flour and maple syrup retrieved from the Mountainview cache, fortunately spared by the forest animals, if only because we had hid the cache in a hole in the rock wall.

"Let's keep these for breakfast tomorrow," he teased.

A mutinous protest arose from the rest of us, remembering the fate of our precious biscuits. We sat around the campfire and gobbled up the maple doughnuts, laughing at the pleasure of the sweet treats. Perhaps Bryan was onto something, using food to uplift people's spirits.

July 31 heralded our last morning at Mosquito Camp. When the tents had all been packed, I gave one more lingering look at the waterfall cascading high on the rock face, the sparkling sand under the rays of the sun, the cool water where I had sought comfort. This special place I committed to memory, even though it had the worst mosquitoes. Then we ferried our final loads back to our starting point.

While we awaited our water taxi at Homathko Camp, Chuck allowed us to use the logging camp's kitchen, which pleased Bryan immensely. He prepared pasta with leftover broccoli from the fridge, which we ate on the building's outdoor patio. The fresh vegetables seemed luxurious to us, as did the chairs we were sitting in. Across the patio table, Joe was back to his usual social, chatty self. Stuart was smiling too, looking much more relaxed and carefree. Talk focused on what food and drink we missed most—beer made the top of the list. We toasted each other with our canteens. Any disappointments we felt were our own to work through.

I kept writing in my journal, partly to keep myself occupied but also to try to capture the details of my experience before time washed them away. Now that our expedition was over, I wanted to absorb the muddle of thoughts and feelings I had about the valley.

On our route along the eastern side of the Homathko, it had taken us three weeks to hike forty kilometres to a point just short of the big bend the river took around Landmark Mountain. Our detour over the Heakamie and Jewakwa bridges had added a few kilometres compared to the Mundays' original route, but we had counted on the logging roads to make our progress easier. In contrast, the Munday party, travelling on the west side of the Homathko, had reached the big bend in about a week.[2] The Munday party, too, found their progress through the valley extremely slow. "Every night the map insisted that we had advanced much less than tired bodies declared we had," wrote Don, forerunning our own experience.[3]

Bryan's dream of climbing Mount Waddington he had conjured up with his friend Ron I. was, perhaps, doomed from the start. Our antique-style boots, wooden pack frames, and wool knickerbockers certainly made us look like 1926 explorers, but to succeed, we required a lot more than dressing the part. The Homathko River Valley remained as wild and unforgiving as it had ever been, and we were hobbled in more ways than one. We hadn't anticipated losing a third of our team, nor that our packs might break under the weight of our belongings; we couldn't believe how impassable was the bush, how challenging to find our way through the valley. Endless delays were lengthened by disruptive arguments among our team borne of frustration and conflicting motivations.

I smiled wryly, remembering the chaotic, muddy start to our adventure. Though our team was united in its passion for climbing, having only recently met, we lacked close-knit friendship. As team leader, Bryan understood the need to choose people who were committed to the historical aspect of our re-enactment, yet he neglected to nurture the bonds among the crew members and align our goals. I struggled to find my voice within a group in which communication was confrontational, secretive, or altogether absent. Joe expressed his disappointments many times on the trail, but they were pleas shouted into the wind. The conflicts among our team haunted us until our final bittersweet toast of rum signalled the end of our troubles. An expedition to Mount Waddington, I learned, required more than physical endurance: just as important were compassion, forgiveness, and a commitment to achieving more together than any one of us could do alone. Don and Phyllis Munday formed a rare partnership. Don depended on Phyllis as his equal, writing, "She and I formed a climbing unit amounting to something more than the sum of our worth apart."[4]

Perhaps our team could have reached Mystery Mountain if we had fostered greater harmony within the group—and if we had been more prudent in our preparations. Before the Mundays' 1926 expedition, they had the foresight to make reconnaissance trips into the valley, leave food caches along the river, and design an effective packaging system for their provisions. Comparing this to our supermarket shopping spree one day before we set sail on the *Misty Isles*, it was clear that we'd taken shortcuts. We'd stuffed our homemade packs to capacity and headed out on the trail in the same way we would with high-tech backpacks. So accustomed were we to modern gear, we hadn't imparted enough importance on field-testing the reliability of our 1920s-style equipment, nor on the logistics involved in moving forward the sheer bulk and weight of the supplies we carried. We required a better organizational system to avoid the constant packing and unpacking of food and to protect it from wildlife. Our provisions, tents, sleeping bags, clothes, and boots were all that protected us from the elements; we needed them to survive in the wilderness. Of course, we knew that if we got into trouble we could hit Greg's emergency button and be plucked out of the bush in a matter of minutes. The Mundays had no such luxury and needed to be completely self-sufficient. For this reason their year comprised two seasons: climbing season and preparation for climbing season.[5]

Though the Mundays' first attempt to find Mystery Mountain plunged through the Homathko River Valley, over the course of a decade they navigated the area from different approaches, through other valleys and up other glaciers. In 1928, their highest point was reaching the lower northwest summit of Mount Waddington, later measured at 13 123 feet (4000 metres). The pinnacle rising before them at 13 186 feet (4019 metres) remained unclimbable. Don described it as "a nightmare moulded in rock."[6] And yet, the Mundays returned to the Waddington Range, year after year. What had started out as a quest to find Mystery Mountain turned into a lifelong passion for exploring the heart of the Coast Mountains.[7]

Even the founding president of the Alpine Club of Canada, Arthur Wheeler, did not at first believe Don's claims about the geography of Mystery Mountain and its surroundings.[8] Using expedition photographs and a compass, Don created detailed topographical maps so impressive, the governing board accepted his recommendations for the names of a number of peaks and glaciers around Mount Waddington before any official survey had been made.[9] In recognition of the Mundays' contributions, in 1928 the board designated a mountain adjacent to Waddington as Mount Munday (elevation 11 500 feet, 3505 metres).[10]

The Mundays' legacy extends beyond proving the existence of Mystery Mountain. Don also contributed to the scientific community's understanding of glaciers at a time when geologists were still unsure whether glaciers moved or were static. He reported detailed measurements and observations along with photographs to several scientific societies in Canada and Britain.[11] Phyllis collected rock and insect specimens for national and provincial museums and later focused on alpine flowers.[12] The body of knowledge they left behind is only enhanced by their deep respect for the mountain environment as a whole.

The Mundays' persistence and dedication fuelled the dreams of men like Bryan, Ron, Joe, Stuart, and Patrick; for me, Phyllis remains a legendary heroine. In re-enacting their first expedition to Mystery Mountain, we paid homage to their dauntless spirit of adventure. The Mundays taught me that a goal unachieved is not a wasted endeavour, especially when there is a tremendously wide world out there to explore. As Phyllis said, "It doesn't matter whether it's a storm or sunshine—it's always worth it."[13]

The next morning, we were visited by dense masses of fog clinging to the mountains, hanging over the logging camp, floating on the river. Walking a hundred feet toward the dock, Greg was a muted shadow of himself, his bright red jacket disappearing into the mists. I thought it uncanny that the landscape had shrouded itself on the occasion of our departure, just as it had when we first entered the valley. We had enjoyed bright, sunny weather for all but one day of our expedition. It was as if we needed to cross a threshold. Here were the mists of time gathering between the valley of 1926 and our world back home.

A misty morning greets the team's preparations for their water taxi pickup from Homathko Camp.

When the water taxi emerged from the fog lying low over the Homathko River, we were nearly ready to go. Wooden pack frames, ten-pound sleeping bags, antique ice axes, and heavy coils of hemp rope were piled up on the grass by the dock. As Joe, Stuart, and Bryan moved the last of our gear to the heap, I took photographs of the misty river, of the white-veiled woods and the mountains beyond. Standing on the grassy bank, on the brink of the wilderness, the whole expedition suddenly seemed extraordinary, like a long trip through the pages of an adventure story. I turned the lens of my camera toward myself and took a self-portrait. There I was, wearing my brown bush hat, my red silk scarf peeking out from the collar of my jacket. In the photo I was smiling, and behind my eyes, I finally saw a fearless and courageous woman.

A self-portrait uncovers a flash of fearless Phyl within.

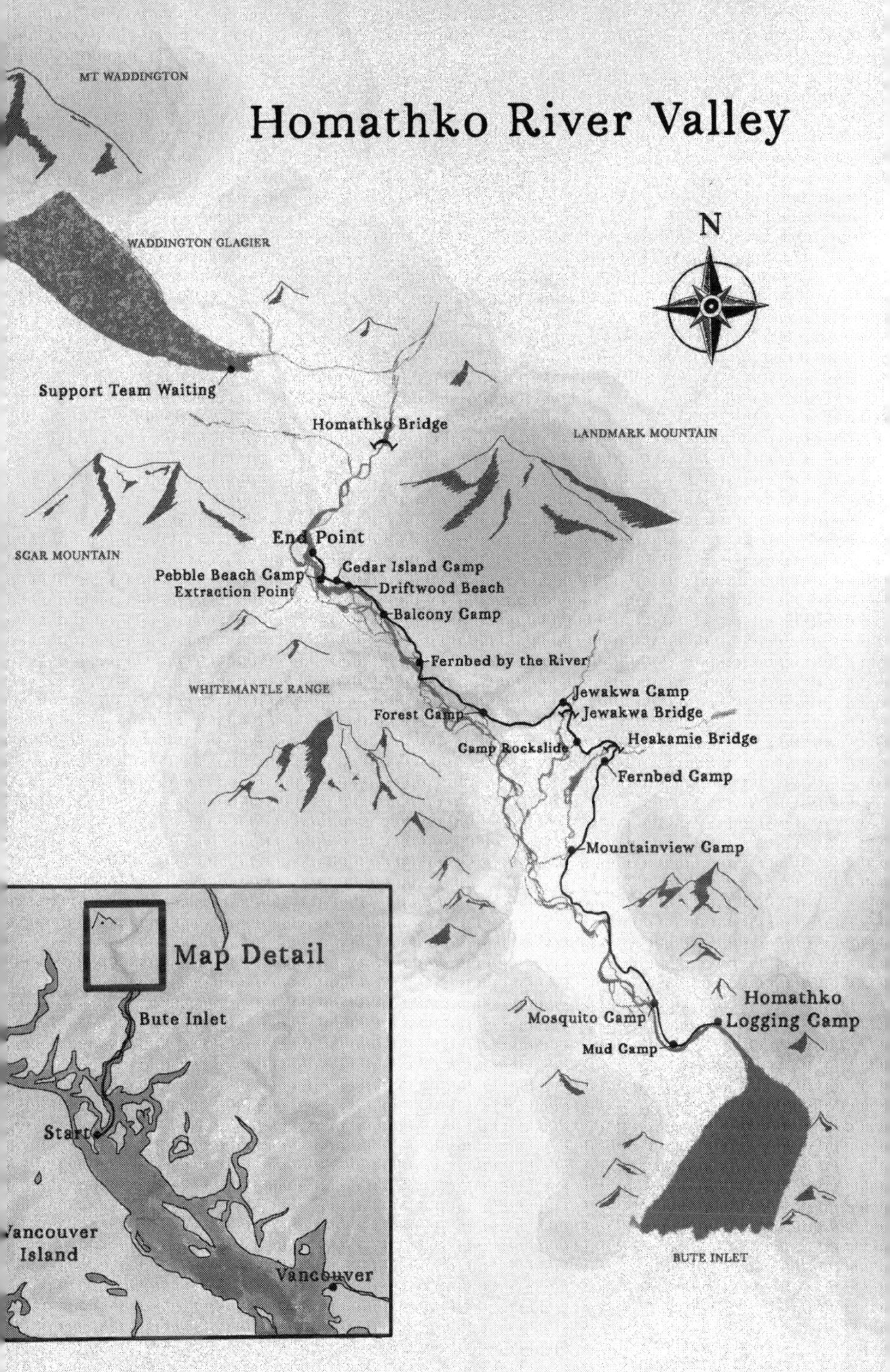

MT WADDINGTON
Homathko River Valley
N
WADDINGTON GLACIER
Support Team Waiting
Homathko Bridge
LANDMARK MOUNTAIN
End Point
SCAR MOUNTAIN
Pebble Beach Camp
Extraction Point
Cedar Island Camp
Driftwood Beach
Balcony Camp
Fernbed by the River
WHITEMANTLE RANGE
Jewakwa Camp
Forest Camp
Jewakwa Bridge
Camp Rockslide
Heakamie Bridge
Fernbed Camp
Mountainview Camp
Map Detail
Bute Inlet
Start
Vancouver Island
Vancouver
Mosquito Camp
Mud Camp
Homathko Logging Camp
BUTE INLET

Acknowledgements

On every journey there are those who accompany us to our summits, whether on roads less travelled or in everyday life. This book would not be possible without the countless people who encouraged and supported me.

It has been my privilege to work with a dedicated and passionate team of people who believed in this book: those who were willing to read my fledgling first drafts, and the second and third ones, and my editor, Laura, who went above and beyond in bringing my story to life; I thank you.

A special thanks to the Canadian EH Society for choosing me to be Phyllis, and to my husband, whose unfailing belief in me gave me strength. I would like to acknowledge the Royal BC Museum Archives for the use of archival images of the Mundays. Recognition is also given to the Xwémalhkwu (Homalco) First Nation, on whose traditional unceded territory our expedition took place.

As I think about the men with whom I spent those memorable few weeks and what we endured together, I am left with a sense of gratitude.

Bryan Thompson

I have received from Bryan a renewed taste for storytelling that may have initiated the idea for this book. His artful skill at making delicious meals out of mundane tins of beans and canned meat amazed me, as did his ingenious hand-built oven. I am grateful for his unwavering belief in me and for keeping an eye on me out there.

Stuart Rickard

From Stuart I learned greater self-sufficiency and woodcraft skills. Thanks to him I know how to make a fire from scratch, chop down trees, and pitch a tent with them. His sewing wizardry got us out of a jam when our pack straps broke, and he made our camp more comfortable by hanging up a tarp for shade or stringing a hammock between two trees. His leadership is an example for us all.

Joe Vanasco

I find myself envious of Joe's openness in expressing his thoughts and feelings. His volubility is something I aspire to. Though not always recognized, his skill in orienteering was invaluable to our team. And from Joe's coffee ritual, I have taken on an appreciation for coffee and good company.

Greg Gransden

Greg helped me remember that my safety in the wilderness is my own responsibility even if I am in a group. His check-ins about where we were on the map were an example to follow. I also valued his suggestions of practical solutions to our troubles, such as gaining more time in the valley by leaving by helicopter. We depended on him as a team member even if he usually stayed quiet behind a camera. His documentary film *The Mystery Mountain Project* is an illuminating window into how our group fared with 1920s-style gear in the remote Homathko River Valley.

Ron Ireland

Though I didn't get to spend much time with Ron I. and Patrick, I do appreciate what they brought to the team. I saw that Bryan's friendship with Ron ran deep, a helpful nudge to treasure my own friends. Patrick I will always remember as the funny guy. A sense of humour, I am reminded, is important to keep in the face of life's challenges.

I hope that this story gives Ron and Patrick a small insight into our experience, for better or for worse.

Bryan, Stuart, Joe, Greg, Ron, and Patrick: forever etched in my memory are your dirty, sweaty faces—and maybe a naked butt cheek or two.

Patrick McGuire

References

Introduction

1. Monica Jackson and Elizabeth Stark, *Tents in the Clouds: The First Women's Himalayan Expedition* (Seattle: Seal Press, 2000), 23.
2. Kathryn Bridge, *Phyllis Munday: Mountaineer* (Montreal: XYZ Publishing, 2002), location 534 of 2064, Kindle.
3. Karen Routledge, "'Being a Girl Without Being a Girl': Gender and Mountaineering on Mount Waddington, 1926-36," The British Columbian Quarterly, no. 141 (Spring 2004): 34, https://doi.org/10.14288/bcs.v0i141.1703.
4. Don Munday, *The Unknown Mountain* (Lake Louise: Coyote Books, 1993), 4.
5. Angus M. Gunn, "Behind the Unknown Mountain," in *The Unknown Mountain* (Lake Louise: Coyote Books, 1993), xix.
6. Robert Friedel, "Zipper," LoveToKnow Corp, accessed April 22, 2020, https://fashion-history.lovetoknow.com/clothing-closures-embellishments/zipper.
7. Bridge, location 999.
8. Kelley McMillan, "Controversy Over 'All-Female' Summit of K2—Men Aided Climb," National Geographic, August 7, 2014, https://www.nationalgeographic.com/adventure/article/140807-k2-women-nepal-pakistan-mountain-summit-controversy.
9. Jennifer Jordan, *Savage Summit: The True Stories of the First Five Women Who Climbed K2* (New York: HarperCollins, 2005), xii.

10. Delphine Moraldo, "Gender relations in French and British mountaineering," Journal of Alpine Research 101-1 (2013), https://doi.org/10.4000/rga.2027.

Chapter One · The First Glitch

1. Bridge, location 1440.
2. Pioneighbour, "Phyllis Munday part 1," YouTube, September 21, 2008, https://www.youtube.com/watch?v=TwYykRd1HCk.
3. Routledge, 38.
4. Bridge, location 924.
5. Canadian War Museum, "FWW_A5_Puttees" (PDF), https://www.warmuseum.ca/s3/supplyline/assets/fwwdiscoverybox/FWW_A5_Puttees.pdf.
6. Bridge, location 1427.
7. Bridge, location 1168.

Chapter Two · The Edge of Civilization

1. Bridge, location 1496.
2. Bridge, location 1502.
3. Routledge, 40.
4. Munday, 132.
5. Munday, 132.
6. Gunn, xx.
7. *Eaton's Catalogue, Spring and Summer 1936* (Toronto: T. Eaton Co., 1936): 189, https://www.bac-lac.gc.ca/eng/discover/postal-heritage-philately/canadian-mail-order-catalogues/Pages/item.aspx?PageId=6822&.
8. Routledge, 44.

Chapter Three · From Disarray to Chaos

1. Gunn, xix.
2. "Tricouni," Outdoor Gear Coach, accessed March 27, 2021, https://www.outdoorgearcoach.co.uk/tricouni-nails/.
3. Munday, 88.
4. Munday, 132.
5. Bridge, location 1563.
6. Bridge, location 1490.
7. Bridge, location 1496.
8. Munday, 25.
9. Munday, 35.
10. Bridge, location 1327.

Chapter Five · Tears and Fears

1. Bridge, location 1435.
2. Munday, 254.
3. Bridge, location 2064.

Chapter Six · The Murky Middle

1. Munday, 121.
2. Munday, 59.
3. Munday, 68.
4. Munday, 55.

Chapter Seven · Unspoken Bonds

1. Munday, 52.
2. Munday, 57.
3. Bridge, location 1423.
4. Munday, 37.
5. Munday, 1.

6. Gunn, xv.
7. Munday, 1.
8. Bridge, location 1550.
9. Bridge, location 1556.

Chapter Eight · A Day Off

1. Munday, 51.
2. Munday, 121, 213.

Chapter Nine · Torment and Surrender

1. Bethany Lindsay, "B.C. Wildfires: Thick smoke grounds firefighting aircraft," CBC News, August 20, 2018, https://www.cbc.ca/news/canada/british-columbia/bc-wildfires-august-20-1.4791637.
2. Munday, 66.

Chapter Ten · Fearless

1. Gunn, xxix.
2. Munday, 42.
3. Munday, 41.
4. Munday, 59.
5. Bridge, location 1454.
6. Bridge, location 1402.
7. Bridge, location 1409.
8. Gunn, xxi.
9. Gunn, xxi.
10. Bridge, location 1473.
11. Bridge, location 1467.
12. Gunn, xxi.
13. Bridge, location 1409.

About the Author

Susanna Oreskovic is a photographer and an adventurer at heart. She was born on a farm at the foot of the Velebit Mountains of Croatia before her family emigrated to Australia, then to Canada. She studied art and sociology before working up the finance career ladder. A dedicated advocate for nature and wild spaces, Susanna lives in Montreal with her husband, three kids, and two cats.

Manufactured by Amazon.ca
Bolton, ON